Effective Instructional Strategies for Cognitive Development

Dr. Shakuntla Nagpal

RAJAT
PUBLICATIONS
New Delhi, India

EFFECTIVE INSTRUCTIONAL STRATEGIES FOR COGNITIVE DEVELOPMENT

This edition is published by Rajat publications
4740/23, Ansari Road Daryaganj,
New Delhi - 110002

ISBN 978-81-87317-98-2

Edition 2026

Printed and bound in India

RAJAT
PUBLICATIONS

4740/23, Ansari Road, Daryaganj,
New Delhi- 110002 (India)
Tel:- +91-11-23267924
Mob:- +91-9811484973, +91-9811105389
E-mail: rajat_publication@yahoo.com

Dedicated

to the

DR MAHENDRA JEET KAUR

Teacher in

Kendriya Vidyalaya

PREFACE

In many ways, this experimental study makes substantial departure from the experimentation that is carried out in the field of education and particularly in the field of cognitive learning. As a matter of fact though it appears that the study has been designed to determine the effectiveness of instructional material prepared on the rationale of Objective Based Teaching and Rapprochement but the major intention has been to empirically validate the basic assumptions propounded by Behaviourists and Cognitive Development Theorists in the development of mental processes. Therefore, this investigation deals with many aspects of problem at hand: First; it provided the experimental findings with regards to the relative effectiveness of Objective Based Teaching and Rapprochement on the development of concepts of science i.e., Achievement in Science and Creativity. Second; a detailed analysis of the concept of Achievement, on the basis of two empirical evidence obtained has been done. Third; a detailed analysis of 'Creativity' as a dependent variable, on the basis of the empirical evidence obtained has been done. Fourth; an effort has been made to explore the world of reality right in the classroom. As a result this research has grown in interaction with real classroom situations not in an isolated laboratory. Endeavours had been made to test the ideas and practices of Objective Based Teaching and Rapprochement to bridge the gap between theory and practice. Fifth; the study tried to explore many unknown relationships, i.e., relationship of Self-concept, Socio-economic Status, Memory and Intelligence to Achievement and Creativity. Sixth; a very little work has been done to study the interrelationships of self-concept, Socio-economic Status, Memory and Intelligence at the elementary level. Researchers find difficult to work with kids. The present investigations by exploring these relationships filled the unfilled gap in the area too. In fact, a learner centred instructional strategy has been evolved for acclerating achievement through higher order thinking.

I am grateful to all those who have helped me in one way or other while carrying out this research. I am also thankful to Rajat Publications for timely publication of the work.

Shakuntla Nagpal

CONTENTS

1

INTRODUCTION

Education is a multidimensional process. It covers the entire gamut of child's life. Not to be confused with either schooling or instruction, education must be considered as a process for the around development of child's personality. During the period of his growth, child must be helped to develop his intellectual, social and moral qualities through a systematic and organised effort in school. We talk today of a learning society. This implies that those who have exposed to educational experiences of some worth will continue to value learning and its outcomes. In order to pave the way for the learning society, it is necessary to point out the current problems and issues that face education in our country. A variety of issues relating to curriculum, teacher-education, guidance, evaluation, education of gifted, and teaching strategies for the development of creative potential among school children are of concern of everybody.

Role of Cognitive Abilities

It is now generally accepted that the major task of education in present society, which is characterised by sudden and rapid changes, is to develop creative potential among the children so that they may successfully respond to and take appropriate action in a variety of situations, which result from quick and successive changes taking place in society in his own life time. With the quantum jump in the knowledge and the fast technological advancement, it is now being realised that creative potential among children should be nurtured in the classroom at early stage. This would enable them to adjust and readjust in the fast changing world in which they live today.

Researches in the area of cognitive abilities have brought to the fore the experience of mental factors which seem to fall broadly under two heads : namely, convergent and divergent thinking. It has also been proved that the divergent thinking abilities constitute a very important cognitive component of creativity. These get stultified when not properly cared for and stimulated. It is, therefore, but essential that in our educational programme, we must attend to the cultivation of these thinking abilities at all levels.

Teaching is objective exploration and symbolic allegorical expression. Competence in teaching can be expressed in terms of teacher's ability to reach out to a heterogeneous group of children by creating a multidimensional environment for them. So, there is a need to develop such instructional design which describes the process of specifying and producing particular environmental situations which cause the students to interact in such a way that specific change occurs in their behaviour.

The present era is an era of science. Every aspect of man's life has been affected by scientific development. Every individual should understand the fundamentals of nature and significance of science in order to lead a wholesome life.

According to the "National Policy on Education (1986)", special emphasis is given to Mathematics and Science education. There is no denying the fact that it is these two subjects, which if taught properly in the early years of child's life can lay the foundation of thinking, reasoning and imagining mind.

In order to achieve the major objectives of teaching the mere book reading and rote memory has to be replaced by the strategies which revolve around two phrases, i.e., "Science is doing" and "Science is life". Creation of learning situation, therefore, becomes one of the fundamental strategies for teaching. Another important strategy for teaching is to relate scientific facts to every day life. These strategies of teaching are amenable by various methods of teaching.

At this juncture to fulfil the requirements of the nation, creative potential and the concepts of environmental education should be developed in the classrooms through a systematically organized programme of instruction.

In ancient days, the emphasis was laid on dogmas; cramming reproduced crammed information and educationists justified their position in teaching the students same in place of natural and harmonious development of their personality. As the understanding of human thinking, especially in the field of cognitive psychology and behavioural psychology developed, new methods and theories emerged out to educate children. Right starting from Thornlike's law of learning (1903), Watson (1913), Pavlov (1927), Skinner (1963), a good account of researches advanced in the field of behavioural psychology are available. Similarly, a great deal of importance has been assigned to the work advanced in the field of cognitive psychology by Piaget (1920 -1980), Bruner (1960) and Ausbel (1960, 62, 68, 78).

The evolution of learning theories gave insight to evolve new approaches of instructions what are termed as teaching learning strategies. Recently two approaches in this field have become very popular, behaviouristic and cognitive theorists, both are based on theories of learning. The efficacy of these two most common approaches in teaching learning process, of various subjects at various school levels has been verified in the educational environment.

Behaviouristic Theory

According to Behaviouristic theory, knowledge exists in the external environment and it must be transferred to the child little by little until complex ideas are build up. This view holds that children have no knowledge for internal structure, hence, it is important to simplify and carefully plan early experiences. Hence, instructions based on behavioural principles are more precise and structured.

According to Behaviouristic theory, Objective Based Teaching provides a theoretical framework, which could be used to improve teaching learning process. This instructional strategy is concerned with the development of intellect through pre-planned objective based instructional and evaluation material, designed for use in teaching with a focus on the development of mental processes.

Objectives, instructions and evaluation are interrelated in the total educational process. The objectives give direction to the instructional methods and curricular content, evaluation seeks to ascertain the degree to which the objectives have been attained collectively for the individual student and for the class as a whole. Dave et al., (1976) developed a model known as *Advanced Curriculum Model of Cognitive-Ledrning* (ACMCL) and derived a hierarchical learning consisting of four educational objectives, i.e., Knowledge, Understanding, Application and Creativity, with 17 mental abilities in term of Expected Behavioural Outcomes (EBO's) and Real Learning Outcomes, (RLO's).

Objective based teaching strategy is three dimensional paradigm and can be represented as

The Input ×	The Process	=	The Output
(Objectives I and EBO's)	(Materials, Method, Mode Media, LE's)		Evaluation (RLO's)

This model has its origin in Bloom's taxonomy and emphasises all the important aspects of any teaching-learning process. The input, i.e., objectives in terms of Expected Behavioural Outcomes (EBO's), the process, which includes different methods and mode media or Learning Experiences (LE's), to achieve pre - determined objectives and lastly the output, which can be evaluated in terms of Real Learning Outcomes (RLO's) to see whether the objectives of teaching - learning process are achieved or not. This in turn assumes a pre-planned objective based instructional and evaluation material especially designed for use in teaching with a focus on the development of mental process.

Cognitive Development Theory

Cognitive development theorists stress that children's mental processes enable them to construct knowledge as they act on their environment. According to Cognitive Development Theory, knowledge is assumed to reside neither in the environment nor in the organism but to be constructed through the interrelationship of both. Although, the development of intelligence (mental processes) proceeds spontaneously, it can be helped or hindered by the environment. The present world into which children are born is far away from an ideal environment for growing intelligence. Many children enter school, if not with a crippled intelligence, at least with an intelligence that is not well nourished. So the schools should offer such an ideal environment, where child is given freedom to explore with environmental things or objects.

Piaget had been an eminent Genevan empirical epistemologist, biologist, educationist and above all a cognitive theorist. The implications of his ideas are being studied in the teaching of all subjects. Piaget's general theory of cognitive growth has widely influenced many aspects of the school curriculum.

His main function in education had been to provide a

criteria for the development of thinking process on which any learning is based. At primary level, a child enters in concrete operational stage. During this period, child's reasoning process becomes logical in relation to the concrete operations. The present system of education is very conservative. The student is fed with the predigested morsels of knowledge and drilled in answering model question papers. Apparently, in the mind of present day teacher, the cramming of the content and obtaining higher grades is the only aim of education, consequently, the development of intellect is suppressed. We must know that the child is not passive, he is active, curious, dynamic and explorative by nature. It has been proved that development of logical structures, hence intellect, subsequently promotes the development of learning of any concept. So the contributor of the development of thinking process is at the initial stages cannot be ignored.

Piaget had emphasised the role of play in the cognitive development of the children. According to him, games and playful activities are important part and parcel of the child's cognitive development. Play is not only for entertainment, it is essentially a means of learning.

Accordingly, the first job of our elementary schools should be to strengthen the thinking foundation on which any learning is grounded. To do this administrators, teachers and society at large must understand the natural development of the child's mind. Moreover at the early schooling, the aim should be to emphasise and purposefully nourish the thinking capacity of the child by providing various playful activities or games, besides making a child to read and write.

Piagetians generally believe in providing experiences, which are not directly related to the school learning. The spontaneous global intellectual development has been considered the outcome of transfer from related but not identical tasks. The Piagetian theory does not directly deal with the desired task. It emphasises cognitive development in isolation to the set curriculum.

In Indian context, it is very difficult to bring sudden revolution in the sense of shifting the whole classroom into playground for the purpose of cognitive development. But at the same time the weakness of the traditional method of teaching cannot be ignored, which is neglecting basic intellectual development and thus, the purpose of teaching is defeated in itself. Therefore, there is a need of bringing revolutionary changes in the total teaching - learning process.

Focus of Behaviourists and Cognitive Theorists

The fundamental focus of behaviourists and cognitive theorists is to stimulate development of intellect. Piagetians aim to develop intellect through action oriented teaching and the aim of behaviourists has been to achieve that goal through pre-planned objective based instructional and evaluation material, while giving due importance to content, input and process interaction variables.

Rapprochement of Objective Based Teaching (OBT) and Piagetian Method of Teaching (PMT)

It is evident from the foregoing discussion that the basic concern of behaviourists and cognitive theorists is the cognitive development. It is also manifested that both have been emphasising interaction among material, mode media to develop intellect, though the nature of material, mode media are different. Since the focus of both is same, therefore these two paradigms could be merged into one and their impact could be simultaneously. Piagetians focused more on teaching - learning process, which get guidance and direction from the predetermined objectives of curriculum and further the effectiveness of that could be simultaneously tested by Real Learning Outcomes (RLO's).

So the rationable of Piaget could be easily incorporated during teaching learning process.

Lunzer (1976) once remarked: "One of the principle objectives in the study of cognitive development may now be to bring about a rapprochement between Genevan approach and that of New Behaviourists (Bloom, Carroll, Gagne and others). On the one hand, it may be fruitful to view the spontaneous development of operational behaviour as the outcome of transfer from related but not identical tasks. On the other hand, it seems essential to supplement the kind of hierarchical conceptualisation as envisaged by Gagne, a hierarchy based on relevant previous knowledge by studying the complementary role of the Piagetian hierarchy, which deals not so much with the knowledge relevant to success in a particular task, as with the way in which these elements need to be fused together to enable the subject to cope with more complex relations."

Nagpal (1983) studied the comparative impact of both these approaches. The result of that study suggested the merger of these two teaching paradigms into one as Piagetians stressed more on active teaching-learning process, which get guidance and direction from preformulated objectives of curriculum and further the effectiveness of that could simultaneously be tested by RLO's. The ACMCL (a behaviouristic model) is a three dimensional paradigm, where the theoretical rationale of Piaget could easily be incorporated in teaching-learning process. As per the rationale of ACMCL a teacher is supposed to plan a few objectives in terms of EBO's in relation to the content. Now in order to achieve these EBO's a teacher may teach through demonstration or concrete examples. Every important concept may be illustrated through pictures, diagrams or models rather than merely through verbal question-answer discussion. Teachers learn to strive to illustrate their verbal presentation through concrete demonstration which lead to stimulating question-answer session. The developed concepts were further evaluated by RLO's. Thus both methods coincided".

Mahinder (1989) could be studied the impact of this approach. Results were every encouraging. The efforts were made to further validate the efficacy of the same.

Yadav (1989) referred to this type of paradigm in the following words - "There is a need of explicit focus to formulate sound and better theory of instructional design through relevant research and it subsequently be done based on valid research design and predecided theoretical framework. For this purposes there is need of combining methodology of teaching with learning process". He further states that "At primary level (lower KG to V Grade) the students be taught through appropriate selection of content. Keeping in view the age, I.Q. and habits of the learner. More specially speaking, one should pay attention on mental maturity of the learner while teaching".

It is very clear from the above discussion that there is a need of having some synchronised curriculum model based on sound theoretical framework which should combine methodology of teaching with learning process. It is also suggested to have activity based method of teaching or Child Centred Instructional Strategy for accelerating learning through higher order thinking.

Hence synchronised Child Centred Instructional Strategy having following characteristics is developed for accelerating learning through higher order thinking among school children.

- It is based on sound theoretical framework of behaviourism.
- It is a combination of methodology of teaching could be with the learning process.
- It is an activity based teaching paradigm.

- It respects the teaching methods for science of thinking and science for thinking.
- The selection of content is sequenced hierarchically from familiar to unfamiliar from the text book itself.
- It ensures a closer correspondence between the curriculum objectives and the content of text book.
- This model fulfils the recommendations of National Policy on Education (NPE) and is relevant in Indian setting.

It has also some following salient features:

1. It is a combination of Objective Based Teaching (OBT) Behaviourism and Cognitive theory.
2. Objective Based Teaching is three dimensional paradigm. It contains - the input -Expected Behavioural Outcomes (EBO's), Method/Mode Media - Learning Situations (LE's) and the output - Real Learning outcomes (RLO's).
3. Piagetian pattern is incorporated at the second level. In teaching - learning process, a few objectives are determined as EBO's. To achieve these objectives, instructions are undertaken according to the rationale of PMT. And the developed concepts are further evaluated by RLO's.
4. This approach is different from demonstration. In demonstration method, there is no clear cut planning of teaching - learning process as the aim of objectives are not specified in observable form.
5. It is step toward cognitive acceleration through science education, which aim to improve children's thinking processes by accelerating progress towards higher-order thinking skills.
6. Demonstration method is a part of this whole paradigm, which is incorporated at the second level of OBT.
7. The whole content of any subject was converted into

appropriate stimulus-response pattern. [Stimulus may be an activity or a verbal question which can stimulate thinking process of the child and motivate him to take active part in learning.]

8. This strategy evaluates the performance of students as Real Learning Outcomes (RLO's) simultaneously. The demand for evaluation of performance arises both from a need for transparency in a democratic society and from the necessity, on the part of educational managers, to as certain the situation of a school system in order to suggest improvements. The transaction of curriculum through this strategy may faculitate the task of evaluators and teachers at the classroom level. This may also help in identifying proper standards and indicators of quality, which is a concern as expressed by educationists of 20 countries in a meeting of International Bureau of Education (IBE) held in Malta in November, 1999.*

Need and Justification of the Study

Nowadays, Educationists are extremely concerned about the deterioration in the educational standards and are sincerely trying to bring about overall improvement in education. For an effective transaction of curriculum, it has been emphasized that a teacher should use a variety of techniques, which would be relevant to the teaching of different types of content and achievement of different instructional, developmental and social objectives of education. Particular emphasis has been laid on those techniques which would ensure pupil participation. Here, it is important to emphasise that Behaviouristic theory as well cognitive development theory fulfil this objective of National Policy of Education (NPE). The New

---

* The IBE/MED Network "Educational Innovation and Information Number 102, March, 2000 IBE, P.O. Box 199, 1211, Geneva, 20, Switzerland.

Educational Policy has come out with an evaluation schedule, which is meant to help the pupil to make continuous progress in all his education endeavour. This is to be noted here that (Real Learning Outcomes) of objective based teaching fulfils this requirement of quality education.

The policy makers have also recognised the importance of evaluating both the scholastic and non-scholastic aspects of educational attainment. The evaluation of cognitive and non-cognitive areas and skill have also been emphasised. Thus the impact of instructional strategies on the development of higher order skills is very important in this context.

Various models of teaching have emerged currently and educationists are awaiting research evidences indicating their potential for effectiveness. Thus the justification of the present model, which is relevant for the present scenario of teaching-learning having research evidences for its potential effectiveness.

Other Dimensions

A student sample in an actual school setting was employed, as it is more favourable to use realistic school situation in order to generalise research findings. Unfortunately, it is very difficult for school teachers and administrators to cater completely to the wishes of researcher regarding the manipulation of students, so it is impractical for researcher to work out a tight research design. In order to make study scientific, it is important to control many confounding variables. The matching operation on many related variables reduces the size of the sample since many students cannot be properly matched on all variables. In such a situation, the data on many possible confounding variables are collected and analysed through statistical control. Keeping in view these research relevant points in mind, variables as socio-economic status; memory and self-concept were included. However, the primary aim of the investigation has been to determine the relative efficacy of Rapprochement, Objective Based Teaching and Traditional Method of Teaching as independent variables on Achievement and Creativity in order to evolve child centred instructional strategy for accelerating learning.

Achievement is generally referred to as the attainment in any subject area. Achievement is a very complex phenomenon and is dependent on a number of factors. It is affected by all types of traits within the individual, and the environment. Many investigators had tried to understand the complexity of this phenomenon, but still it is not fully understood. Various organismic and environmental factors play an intricate role in explaining the variance in achievement.

According to *Warren's Dictionary of Psychology* (1934), "Achievement is proficiency of performance generally measured by a standard task or test".

Academic achievement is explained as "knowledge attained or skill developed in a school subject, usually designed by test scores, by marks assigned by teacher or by both".

There are various methods designed to measure the individual achievement against a specific achievement norm (standard) e.g. achievement batteries or achievement tests.

An achievement test measures the extent to which a person has achieved something, acquired certain information or mastered certain skills, usually as a result of specific instruction.

Thus an achievement test measures the performance of the pupils which they have acquired as a result of some specific methods of teaching.

Achievement is operationally defined as the development of concepts with respect to the levels of learning, i.e., knowledge, understanding and application and achievement, with the help of the content of the prescribed text book, as a result of teaching strategies. Level of learning identified as Knowledge, Understanding and Application are operationally defined as follows:

Knowledge

Knowledge is defined as recall and recognition of facts, figures, symbols, letters and words.

Understanding

Understanding means the mental process of seeing relationship, citing examples, discrimination, classification, interpretation, verification and generalisation.

Application

Application involves the ability to use information, ideas, concepts, rules, methods or processes to deal with a practical problem not encountered before. It further involves the mental process of reasoning, hypothesising, inferring and predicting.

Creativity

Today our country is facing tremendous problems on the other hand fast and rapid technological advancement are taking place throughout the world. Further, the challenges of 21st century have to be met. Therefore, the creative talents for the country are needed to be developed. Such leaders have to be produced, who do not fall back on the old pattern of thinking but persons with vision who could boldly face the problems and find solutions to the challenges. Therefore, it is the task before educators to identify, encourage and develop creative talents.

Moony has described four approaches to creativity in terms of 4 P's

1. Creative Product

2. Creative Process

3. Creative Person

4. Creative Press (Environment).

According to the Moony's fourth approach to the creativity, creative process can be nourished in healthy environment. Teaching-learning process can stimulate this ability and help students to develop this potential to its maximum.

Creativity is a multidimensional attribute. Generally the most widely used conception of creativity are formulated either in terms of some manifest product (like painting, poem) or any underlying process (aesthetic judgement). Creativity has been variously defined.

Piers et al. (1960), remarked about creativity as the capacity of the individual to avoid usual routine and conventional ways of thinking and doing things.

Guifford (1956) defined creativity as the process variable by distinguishing divergent thinking behaviour from convergent thinking.

Guilford (1956), Sultan (1962), Anderson (1964) and Taylor (1964) explained the construct through factor analytical approach and thought of the possibilities of different factors being involved in the construct of the creativity.

Drevdahl (1956) defined creativity as the capacity of the person to produce composition, products or ideas of any sort which are essentially new or novel and previously unknown to the producer.

Torrance (1962) focused on creativity as a process of becoming sensitive to problems, deficiencies, gaps of knowledge, missing elements, disharmonious and so on, identifying the difficulty; searching for solution, making guesses or formulating hypotheses about the deficiencies, testing and retesting these hypotheses and possibly modifying and retesting them and finally communicating the results".

Cavé (1970) has tried to define creativity in what could be described through creativity tests measuring fluency, flexibility, originality and elaboration.

The operational definition of creativity as defined by Torrance. Tests of fluency, flexibility and originality as measured through 'Thinking Creatively with Words' has been considered as appropriate as measures of Creativity in the present context.

The impact of teaching methods was observed in the development of creativity through fluency, flexibility and originality.

Objective Based Teaching

The concept of Objective Based Teaching has been derived from Advanced Curriculum Model of Cognitive Learning (ACMCL), which provide a theoretical framework to improve teaching-learning process. This model had its origin in Bloom's Taxonomy of educational objectives; Cognitive Domain (1956), which had generated a lot of enthusiasm among the curriculum workers all around the world. According to Bloom's Taxonomy the educational objectives have classified into three domains.

1. Cognitive Domain
2. Affective Domain
3. Psychomotor Domain.

In teaching-learning process cognitive aspects are emphasised more. The Cognitive Domain has been classified into six categories, namely, Knowledge, Comprehension, Application, Analysis, Synthesis and Evaluation, ranging from simple to the most complex cognitive processes. Bloom's taxonomy served as model for further taxonomies like Affective Domain Model of

Krathwhol (1964), Psychomotor Domain Model of Simpson (1966) and Harrow (1972), Experiential Domain Model of Steinker (1975), ACMCL of Dave (1976) and three hierarchical models of Reading Comprehension by LAP and Flood (1981). All the taxonomies and related work assumed hierarchical arrangement of abilities.

Dave *et al.* (1976) derived a hierarchy learning consisting of four educational objectives viz. Knowledge, Understanding, Application and Creativity with Seventeen mental abilities in terms of Expected Behavioural Outcomes (EBO's) and Real Learning Outcomes (RLO's). It is be described as follows :

1. **Knowledge**
    - Recognition
    - Recall
2. **Understanding**
    - Seeing relationship
    - Citing examples
    - Discriminating
    - Classification
    - Interpretation
    - Verification
    - Generalisation
3. **Application**
    - Reasoning
    - Formulating hypothesis
    - Establishing hypothesis
    - Inference
    - Prediction

4. Creativity

- Analysis
- Synthesis
- Judgement

The Advanced Curriculum Model of Cognitive Learning (ACMCL), is diagrammatically represented as :

The input (Objectives and EBO's)	×	The process (Material, Methods, Mode Media) (LE's)	=	The output (Evaluation) (RLO's)

As depicted above this is a process oriented teaching-learning behavioural model, where those behaviours are developed which are intended as the end product of learning through deliberate and planned instructional efforts. The process of teaching is integrated with learning outcomes (product), and learning outcomes are linked to teaching-learning process and to the objectives expected to be attained. The concept of Objective Based Teaching is derived from this in which due importance is given to the input, the process and the output.

The following are the implied assumptions of Objective Based Teaching (O B T).

1. The development of the mental abilities should be the goal of teaching process.
2. They should be clearly stated in terms of Expected Behavioural Outcomes (EBO's) of pupils.
3. Learning Experiences (LE's) should be provided with reference to (EBO's) only.
4. No learning experiences, no change in behaviour can be expected.

5. Real Learning Outcomes (RLO's), i.e., evaluation depend upon the quality of learning experiences.
6. Learning experiences consist of dynamic interaction among teachers, pupils and media / materials.
7. Multiway interaction among teachers, materials and media intensify and accelerate higher levels of learning.

To fulfil these assumptions, deliberate teaching of the content is to be undertaken for the development of Expected Behavioural Outcomes (EBO's) before evaluating the product. This in turn assumes a pre-planned objective based instructional and evaluation material is to be especially designed for use in teaching with a focus on the development of mental processes.

Synchronisation of Objective Based Teaching Paradigm and Piagetian Method of Teaching Paradigm into Pragmatic Child Centred Instructional Strategy

Rapprochement is the Synchronisation of Objective Based Teaching and Piagetian Method of Teaching resulting into pragmatic instructional Strategy.

Piagetian Method of Teaching

Piaget has been the most outstanding exponent of the cognitive development approach. Piaget's most significant contribution to contemporary educational thought and practice had been his theory of specific intellectual developmental stages in children. He was concerned with the qualitative changes taking place in a person's mental make up from birth to maturity. The human organism, like all other biological entities has a characteristic internal organisation, which is responsible for the organism's unique mode of invariant functioning. The three postulates, *i.e.*, internal organisation, invariant functions and interaction between organism and environment have been fundamental to Piaget's position.

His theory deals with the nature and development of thinking. It's main function in education has been to provide a criterion for the development of thinking process on which any learning is based.

Following Points Highlight the Views of Piaget

1. Cognitive development results through biological maturation, interaction with the environment and equilibration. Heredity and maturation are not the prime causes of development of intelligence, therefore, there is need to provide an environmental setting to the child, which is favourable to activate thinking in a direct and theoretically well motivated fashion.
2. The general development of intelligence is the basis on which any specific learning depends. Learning can only take place on condition that the child has general mechanism to which he can assimilate the information contained in learning. In this sense intelligence is the most necessary instrument of learning. So the learning aspect and the thinking aspect can not be separated.
3. Intelligence and thinking are synonymous. Thinking stands for active use of intelligence. Intelligence is the instrument by means of which a person thinks.
4. Intelligence and creativity are not two separate entities but are closely related to each other. Intelligence is constructive and creative when the development of intelligence is the gradual creation of new mechanisms of thinking. It is creation because it is the discovery not the copy of anything that is physically present.
5. The child is an active, curious, dynamic and explorative. At primary level, a child enters in concrete operational stage. During this period, child's reasoning process becomes logical in relation to concrete operations. Piaget had emphasised the

role of play in the cognitive development of the children. Games and playful activities are important part and parcel of the child's cognitive development. Play is not only for entertainment, it is essentially a means of learning.

The need to develop thinking process of the child at initial stage is important, as all types of learning is based on the thinking. At the concrete operational stage, a child reasons successfully about things that are or have been concretely presented to him. Accordingly, the main aim of elementary schools is to provide an environmental setting which is favourable for the development of thinking process of the child. A number of researches have been carried out in this field and a number of tasks have been developed by many researchers in relation to the cognitive development of the child. It is to be noted that these efforts have not been directly related to the child's school learning, Hence, they are not accepted readily in this sense as they provide a criterion for the development of intellect in isolation. There is need to relate the Piagetian concept of cognitive development with the school learning itself.

Synchronisation of Objective Based Teaching and Piagetian Method of Teaching

Rapprochement is defined as the harmonious relationship between two paradigms. Basically the aims and objectives of both are same, i.e., intellectual development. Therefore, they are merged into one, evolving a new strategy called *Synchronisation* into pragatic instructional strategy, which is Child Centred.

Objective Based Teaching is derived from the Advanced Curriculum Model of Cognitive Learning (ACMCL), which is a behaviouristic model emphasising an objective based instructional and evaluations teaching strategy with due importance to the content or syllabus. This strategy is applicable in the school learning as it involves all essential aspects of a teaching learning process, i.e., the input (objectives), the process (instructions, method) and the output (evaluation).

Piagetians believe in the cognitive development of the child through a variety of situations, activities and materials, which enhance the thinking process of the child. These learning aspects are incorporated with the Objective Based Teaching to get a pragmatic instructional strategy. These situations, activities and materials were incorporated at the second level of the OBT, i.e., the process (instructions, methods). Hence in teaching learning process objective were determined. To achieve these objectives instructions were based on Piagetian method of teaching and than the evaluation was done on the basis of OBT, to assess the level of achievement.

2

REVIEW OF LITERATURE

What flows from the past, leads to evolve and propose something meaningful to the present. A survey of the researches conducted and published in the field, extends help in the selection of problem, its planning and execution for the purpose of a research investigation. The search for related studies in this area has been very fruitful as it provided in depth understanding of the type of research work going on in the field. A few studies could be located relating to one part or the other of the problem, Empirical evidences about the effect of culture-specific teaching-learning paradigm on achievement were found lacking. Some theoretical views were available which were used.

Teaching Strategies and Learning Outcomes

The present study is concerned with two types culture specific teaching strategies, they are Objective Based Teaching and Rapprochement. The survey of literature had revealed paucity of controlled experimental evidence in this particular area. However, some studies and theoretical ideas are discussed.

Objective Based Teaching and Learning Outcomes

Educational researches had established the fact that achievement is enhanced in classroom, where children can perceive a sense of direction in learning. This view holds the fact that effective teaching-learning strategies, in which every aspect of this process is equally emphasised would definitely enhance pupil achievement. A number of attempts have been made in formulating such a framework. The importance of objectives of teaching-learning process and formulation of these objectives in behavioural terms have been practised by many curriculum workers.

The most outstanding and internationally known effort made in classification of educational objectives is that of Bloom (1956) and his associates. It was the taxonomy that leads to the movement of specifying the objectives and development of taxonomic, models or paradigms.

Glasser (1962), Magor (1962), Lindvall (1964), Tyler (1964), Walbesser (1964), Krathwahl (1965), Gagne (1966), Popham (1968) emphasised the utility of behavioural objectives as indicators of directions of pupils growth intended learning outcomes.

Magor (1962), Lindvall (1964), Tyler (1964), Walbesser (1964), Gagne (1966), Hasting (1966), Metfesse and Micheal (1969) were among those who expressed objectives in behavioural terms as the only way to describe and evaluate the curriculum development process as well as the end product of curriculum.

Anderson (1964) prepared taxonomy type tests using chemistry material to validate the assumption of behavioural objectives. The factor analysis of pre and post-test scored provided K and C items forming one factor and A and ANA another.

Smith (1965) investigated the scalibility of the K and C levels of taxonomy. The data on 341 students in educational psychology course failed to form a simplex through the use of the Guttman scale.

Knopp and Stoker (1966) made a comprehensive attempt

to validate the assumptions underlying the taxonomy of educational objectives of Bloom. The data obtained were analysed through the Kaiser technique for scaling a simplex, the factor analysis and the Guttman's circumflex analysis. Investigator concluded that scores were determined by highly complex interaction of content and process.

Popham (1968) examined the validity of most of the arguments against behavioural objectives and concluded that by and large all arguments raised against behavioural objectives are insipid, ill-founded and ill-convinced.

Atkin (1968) argued that behavioural objectives may develop a convergent thinking.

Pachaury's (1971) reanalysis of Melgesors's work investigating the relationship between concepts or force attained and maturity as indicated by grade levels, in general supported the cumulative hierarchical structure of taxonomy, but not conclusively as did the study by Knopp and Stoker (1966) and Smith (1985).

Heron (1971) as a result of review of the literature concluded that some studies seem to indicate that by providing students with objectives, achievement will be enhanced.

Dave and Anand (1972), Sharma and Padma (1972-76) attempted to find out the effect of different teaching patterns on the cognitive attainment of pupils. Sharma found that an objective based teaching is more effective than other teaching pattern in attaining the knowledge and comprehension.

Stedman (1973) reported that taxonomy are hierarchically arranged is acceptable only if the hierarchy is viewed as progressive uneven from low cognitive levels to higher cognitive levels.

Arnold, Alwelle and Rogers (1973) reported that levels of questioning is significantly related to the levels of response to question. The study highlighted the use of objective based questions at all levels to improve students' achievement on higher objectives.

Clifford and Sherman (1975) studied the effect of providing students with objectives on achievements. They reported that objective based teaching, cognisance of objective by students and teachers is important to develop different cognitive abilities.

Treffinger and Heber (1975) believed that psychological principles of sound instructional planning can be applied productively to creative problem solving.

Dave (1976) reported that students taught with the help of objective based instructional material showed greater acquisition of Knowledge, Understanding and Application than those taught by the traditional method.

Pritam Singh (1978) has demonstrated the impact of objective based instruction on the achievement of students at secondary level.

Jones and Russell (1979) pointed out that learning paradigms permit the teachers to diagnose limitations and strengths of students effectively and thereby permitting more adequate individualisation and personalisation of instructions. The importance of the subparts (EBO) of the paradigm has been emphasised for providing clues for the development of teaching techniques and strategies which consequently influence the acquisition of skill, knowledge and attitudes.

Manjula (1980) found in that students taught with the help of objective based instructional material had shown significant gain on Achievement in Science and on Creativity than those taught by the traditional method at the elementary level. Jarolimak and

Forster (1981) emphasized the importance of objective based teaching.

Nagpal (1983) found students taught with objective teaching scored higher than those taught by the traditional method.

Vanita (1985) had demonstrated the impact of objective based teaching on the achievement of students at primary level in rural area.

Juna, (1985) in A Comparative Study of Nurturant effect strategy and traditional strategy on the improvement of Learning Abilities in Environment Oriented Primary Science Education Programme concluded that nurturant objective based on instructional strategy is superior to the traditional strategy in the improvement of pupils learning abilities.

Rapprochement and Learning Outcomes

Rapprochement of Objective Based Teaching and Piagetian Method of Teaching is a new technique of teaching, which is experimentally verified for its effectiveness in actual classroom situation. Studies in this particular area are lacking. A few theoretical ideas no doubt have been advocated.

Lunzer (1976), long back while appreciating contributions of Piaget had suggested that one of the principal objectives in the study of cognitive development may be to bring about a rapprochement between the Genevan approach and that of New Behaviourists (Bloom, Carrall, Gangne and Others). On the one hand, it may be fruitful to view the spontaneous development of operational behaviour as the outcome of transfer from the related but not identical tasks. On the other hand, it seems essential tc supplement the kind of hierarchical conceptualisation envisaged by Gagne; a hierarchy based on relevant previous knowledge by studying the complementary role of the Piagetian hierarchy, which deals not so much with knowledge relevant to success in a particular task as with the way in which these elements need to be fused together to enable the subject to cope with more complex relations".

Brainard (1978) had concluded that "Piaget oriented educators had failed to establish a case for restructuring traditional curricula along Piagetian lines. The evaluation data on the Piagetian projects had failed to show any differences between Piagetian instructions and other curricula. There is good reason to believe that the characteristics of teacher are more crucial than the curricula and the associated educational philosophies. Following changes were suggested in curriculum, "if the learning and thinking models of the children are to be adjusted to the curriculum, the content must be appropriate to the thought structure of the learner at his stage of development."

Nagpal (1983, 1996) has suggested that the two teaching paradigms can be merged into one and their impact on teaching-learning process needs to be tested simultaneously. Piagetians focus more on teaching- learning process which can get guidance and direction from the preformulated objectives and further the effectiveness of that can be simultaneously tested by RLO's. The Objective Based Teaching is a three dimensional paradigms, where the theoretical rationale of Piaget can be easily incorporated at the second level, i.e., in teaching-learning process as per the rationale of Objective Based Teaching a teacher is supposed to plan a few objectives in terms of EBO's in relation to the content. Now in order to achieve these EBO's a teacher may teach through demonstration of concrete examples or activities or games. Every important concept may be illustrated through pictures, diagrams or models rather than merely through pure verbal question-answer discussion. Teachers can learn to strive to illustrate their verbal presentations through concrete demonstration which may lead to stimulating question-answer session. The developed concepts may further be evaluated by Piagetian tasks as well by RLO's. Thus both methods can be coincided and hence a research was carried out to validate both at the same time by Mahinder (1985) to see the efficacy of this Rapprochement, where she found the superiority of this approach.

Supportive Empirical Evidences

Many researchers had experimentally studied the relevance of Piagetian theory and tasks in order to know the development of various concepts among children and adolescents.

Owen (1973) studied basic research in the application of Piagetian Cognitive Development Theory to the curriculum used in the primary school classroom. Small group activities were provided to improve the abilities of the children to use mental processes, which were prerequisite to the development of concept of a number and concluded that these activities along were not effective in enhancing the ability of the students.

Newby (1973) discerned implications for elementary curriculum inherent in Piagets theory for the development of concrete logical thinking. Implications for an elementary school curriculum focused on operational thinking, learner participation and social involvement. Newby concluded that Piaget's research had provided a detailed description of the manner in which a child structure his intelligence to allow logical reasoning. The theory should guide educators in planning elementary school curriculum.

A traditional Headstart programme was carried out by Diamond (1975). With intention to determine whether Pigetian tasks would enhance classification and seriation skills and conservation of discontinuous and continuous qualities in experimental group than in the control group. In order to help students progress from pre-operational to concrete operational through curriculum, Piagetian tasks were added to the daily class routine. The teachers aided in playing with materials physically and verbally. Nine separate activities using a variety of toys were spread over the school years, specifically addressed to seriation, classification and conservation concepts. Building a general climate of inquiry was attempted. Open ended questions encouraged various physical and verbal responses. It was found that seriation skills were developed more in the experimental group than in the control group.

Bingham Newsman (1975) examined the pattern of inducements in cognitive development in 48 children aged 3-5 years and compared the effect of two contrasting pre-school programmes on the development of logical operational ability. The experimental group incorporated a theoretical framework and a teacher educational built on the Piagetian theory. The control group used a conventional nursery school programme. A representative battery of Piagetian tasks and two standardised non-Piagetian measures were administered. Cross sectional analysis demonstrated marked differences between the two groups.

Piagetian models had become prominent particularly among early childhood education. Four major programmes were carried out.

The first model was developed by Celia Lavattele (1970) and was referred to as "Piaget based curriculum for children 4 to 7 years old." It was focused on the concrete operational counts number, space, classification, seriation. The basic idea was to give pre-school children systematic instructions in each of these areas. The underlying assumption was that instructions would help to smooth the way for the transition from preoperations to concrete operations.

The second, David Weikart's (1973) programme, the "Cognitively Oriented Curriculum" designed the entire learning environment on Piagetian Model. This programme was focused on one specific type of correct operational content, i.e., classification. He believed that classificatory skills are especially important for reading arithmetic.

The third was the University of Wisconsin's Piagetian Preschool Education Programme (PPEP) (1974) based on nine instructional guidelines. Pupils were exposed to contents from the concrete operational level. However, the emphasis was on getting children discover these contents by themselves. Most instructional activities consisted of manipulating concrete objects and interacting with other children. PPEP was subjected to a three years comprehensive field evaluation at the University of Wisconsin's Early Childhood Study Centre (Bingham-Newsman, Sounders and Hooper, 1976). The basic question examined was whether a pre-school curriculum based on Piagetian theory facilitates the process of developmental change. At the University, this programme was conceived as an exploratory three years research programme. Though the experimental children made significant gains on the majority of the measures, a few of the comparisons in favour of the control group were significant.

The fourth educational model was that of Kamii and De Vries (1974) "Piaget Based Curriculum for Early Childhood Education." In this, no experimentation is made of the tangible educational goals normally associated with classroom instruction. Daily lesson plans and other features of 'Cook book' curricula were viewed as inconsistent with the true Piagetian approach to teaching. Kamii and De Vries writes about the teacher's job as "to create an environment and an atmosphere conducive to learning; to provide materials, suggest activities and assess what is going on inside the chiid's head from moment to moment; to respond to children in terms of the kind of knowledge involved; and to help the child extend his ideas".

Piagetian primary school programme "Thinking goes to school" by Furth and Wachs (1975) was to aid and nourish the normal developing process of thinking in the primary school child, subordinating all school activities to this first goal. The major aim of the programme was to prepare children for the task of further education and prevention of many academic failures and learning disabilities. The programme was limited to the primary grades because during this period the chiid could form healthy habits of thinking as a foundation for intelligent reading and successful acquisition of all other academic skills. Various games and play sequences were designed to develop the child's thinking ability. The thinking games and activities were supposed to provide a general foundation which should help the child to deal successfully with specific academic subjects. The programme was developed for kindergarten through the third grade. Emphasis was to create thinking environment, where children could live and learn. But this never became a fully developed programme, only lasting from 1970 to June 1972, when originally it was proposed for three years plans. The school which was conceived by Furth and Wachs, was discontinued by the administration. A complaint by Furth and Wachs (1975) states that there was a constant pressure to show-short term results on standard reading tests, and the constant need to justify the programme not on its own terms, but in terms of the traditional philosophy and of immediate results. However, the qualitative results supported the effectiveness of this programme.

Nagpal (1983) tried out the efficacy of Thinking Games developed by Furth and Wachs, Results of the study showed that the students who were exposed to Thinking Games scored higher than those taught by traditional method.

Nagpal and Vanita (1985) further found in an experiment using pre-post test that the students exposed to Thinking Games gained higher scores than those taught by the traditional method in a rural setting in science.

Piagetian tasks had been designed and implemented sparingly in the Indian context. However, Vaidya (1974, 79) developed tasks to assess logical reasoning in science. Nair and Padmini (1980) devised 'Mysore Cognitive Capability Test' for Primary School Children. Chanda (1980), Sandhu (1981), Arya (1981), Amin (1982), Padhy (1986), Ghosh (1986). Pass et al. (1985) developed the Piagetian tasks for the cognitive development of Primary school children, but none have used these tasks as a teaching strategy for development of learning in the class room.

All the above studies revealed that a number of attempts had been made by many researchers to see the efficacy of Piagetian theory and tasks but a very few seemed to be fruitful as these tasks were not directly related to the existing curricula of schools. Hence the scope of Piagetian thinking and its implementation is still lacking in Indian Educational system, the Piagetian approach is incorporated in a different way in a teaching strategy, the feasibility of which is tested in Indian context. The result are in a positive direction.

Teaching Strategies and Creativity

The deteriorating effect of traditional method on the nurturance of creative ability has been reported regularly by one and all.

Torrance (1965) concluded on the basis of field experiments, instructional materials, designed to provide key experiences in creative thinking and containing information about the nature and value of creative process, proved powerful enough to make differences in creative development.

Hallman (1967) had shown that research literature supports the position that creativity can indeed be caught but it cannot be taught by the traditional/authoritarian methods. Creative procedures cannot be prescribed nor can they be written into lesson plans, yet creative teaching is the best way, perhaps the only way, to promote creative behaviour on the part of the pupil. It is suggested that effective teacher must invent his own creative techniques as a part of the specifics, ongoing teaching operation in the classroom. The procedure which is invented will appear in the given situation on having been unforcible and unexpected, as a surprise, their effectiveness will be enhanced. It remains to be investigated whether the principles of creative teaching are identical with the principles of all good teaching. Their creativity will be overlapping for the simple reason that good teaching is creative teaching.

Creative teaching as defined by Frank William (1969) is, what gives rest to learning and provides opportunities and encouragement for causing the child to think and feel. It should not play a minor role in the learning process. Such a learning climate should provide the child with huge experiences and encounters for being imaginative, dealing in fantasy, doing, roaming, wondering, guessing, trying, inquiring, playing around with questions and discrepancies, testing one's idea or generate data against the facts. All of these are ingredients of creativity, which cut across both the cognitive and affective domains. Eble (1969) had stated that there is some reason to believe that educational system can reduce originality and creativity. This negative effect on creativity is most marked when examination, instructional material and processes all emphasize learning by rote and the goal is centred only on getting through examinations.

Still (1970) has stated, "As for as creativity is concerned, teaching and learning are closely interrelated." Creative teachers performance tends to stimulate creative learning and with the result the teachers and students expand potentialities for creativity.

"Creative Teaching" and "Creative Learning" refer to what happens when the pupil becomes involved in the creative learning. Creative ways of learning have built in power motivation the process only has to be encouraged. Further learning primarily involve such abilities as recognition, memory and logical reasoning which are independently, the abilities most frequently assessed by traditional intelligence tests and measures of scholastic aptitude. In contrast, the learning creatively through creative and problem solving activities, in addition to recognition, memory and logical reasoning; requires such abilities as evaluation (especially the ability to sense the problem in consistency and missing elements), divergent production (e.g., flueney flexibility, originality and elaboration) and redefinition.

Lefrancois (1972) had emphasised that the teachers are rigid, rule bound and authoritarian. They stifle creativity in the students by insisting on excessive conformity to arbitrary regulations, giving high grades for neat, correct, unimaginative solutions. Can we teach children to think creatively? Indeed successful approaches do exist which make it possible to teach children to think creatively. Torrance (1973) had shown success in teaching children to think creatively. He concluded that the most popular approach to teaching children to think creatively has been through complex programmes involving packages of materials, the manipulation of teacher classroom variables and the case of modification and of the Training Programme which have shown over 90 per cent success.

Anderson (1974) had described that creativity is in each of us, as small child, among adults it is almost non-existent. The question is what happened to this enormous and universal human resource? The answer lies in the system of education, which is concerned mainly with acquiring a body of knowledge, memorising facts and finding answers to problems all of which are already known to someone else rather than with creativity.

Khire (1977) had remarked that the present educational techniques and curricula aim to meet the requirement of developing a specific kind of cognitive-intelligence. Free, flexible and original thinking, which often departs from the set patterns, does not receive due respect.

Manjula (1980) found that Objective Based Teaching had positive effect on creative components. It is a learner Centred Instructional Strategy aimed at accelerating learning through higher order thinking.

Nagpal (1983) proved that it is positively and significantly related to creativity and traditional method of teaching is not related to any component of creativity.

3

PLAN AND PROCEDURE OF THE STUDY

In this chapter, the aims and objectives of the study, the research design, selection of sample and various steps taken to prepare achievement test are described. The procedure and justification for preparing instructional material for experimental groups has been discussed along with the actual experimental phase. Justification of the selection of instruments for measuring various variables is also described.

Fundamental Assumptions

The study started with the following assumptions:

First; Marks pertaining to the questions of different levels of Learning, i.e., Knowledge (K), Understanding (U) and Application (A) in the Achievement Test are additive.

Second; Scores on creativity tests, pertaining to different components, i.e., Fluency (F), Flexibility (X) and Originality (O) are additive.

Third; Treatment variables, i.e., Rapprochement (Rapp) and Objective Based Teaching (OBT) and Traditional Method of Teaching (TMT) are nominal. They are treated as Dummy Variables.

Fourth; In case of undimensional test of Intelligence scores based on different items are additive.

Fifth; All the relationship which this explored have been assumed to be linear.

Purpose of the Study

Primary Purpose

(1) To study the relative effectiveness of Learner Centred Teaching-Learning Paradigm as Rapprochement, Objective Based Teaching and Traditional Method of Teaching on the Achievement and Creativity at Primary level.

Secondary Purpose

(2) To study the relationship of Creativity components, i.e., Fluency (F), Flexibility (X), Originality (O) and Total Creativity (C) to the Levels of Achievement, i.e., Knowledge (K), Understanding (U), Application (A), Total Achievement (T) and Academic Attainment.

(3) To study the relationship of Memory, Self-Concept, Socio-Economic Status and Intelligence with that of the levels of Achievement, i.e., Knowledge (K), Understanding (U), Application (A), and School Achievement (SA).

(4) To study the relationship of Memory, Self-Concept, Socio-Economic Status, and Intelligence with the Creativity components, i.e., Fluency (F), Flexibility (X), Originality (O),- and Creativity (C).

To achieve the above purpose the following tasks in a sequence were formulated.

Tasks

1. Construction and standardisation of Achievement test.
2. Development of Instructional Material for Experimental groups.

3. Testing experimentally the effectiveness of developed Instructional Material for the Experimental groups.
4. Determining the association of Creativity Components (F,X,O) with School Achievement in terms of higher order thinking.
5. Exploring relationships of Memory, Self-Concept, Socio-Economic Status, Intelligence with School Achievement (SA).
6. Exploring relationship of Memory, Self-Concept, Socio-Economic Status, Intelligence with Creativity.

From the above discussion, purposes and tasks, following hypotheses were formulated.

Hypothesis of the Study

Experimental Hypotheses

1. Significant differences exist among three groups namely, Experimental Group I (Rapprochement), Experimental Group II (Objective Based Teaching) and the Control (Traditional) with respect to Achievement Academic Attainment (SA) and Creativity.
2. Children taught by Rapprochement show higher scores on Achievement, Academic Attainment (SA) and Creativity taught by the Traditional Method.
3. Children taught by Objective Based Teaching show higher scores on Achievement, Academic Attainment (SA) and Creativity in than taught by the Traditional Method.
4. Children taught by Rapprochement show higher scores on Achievement, Academic Attainment (SA), and Creativity in than taught by Objective Based Teaching.

Null Hypotheses

5. There is no relationship of creativity to the Achievements and Academic Attainment.

6. There is no relationship of Creativity to Memory.
7. There is no relationship of Creativity to Self-Concept.
8. There is no relationship of Creativity to Socio-Economic Status.
9. There is no relationship of Creativity to Intelligence.
10. There is no relationship of Achievement and Academic Attainment to Memory.
11. There is no relationship of Achievement and Academic Attainment to Self-Concept.
12. There is no relationship of Achievement and Academic Attainment to Socio-Economic Status.
13. There is no relationship of Achievement and Academic Attainment to Intelligence.
14. There is no relationship among Memory, Self- Concept, Socio-Economic Status and Intelligence.

Design of the Study

A carefully and cautiously structured research design as a pre-requisitic to obtain maximum fruitful benefit from an investigation has been developed. Experimentation is the name given to the type of educational research in which the investigator controls the educative factors to which a child or a group of children are subjected during the period of inquiry and observes the resulting achievement. The experimental method in educational research is the application and adoption of the classical methods of science laboratory. It is the most exact and difficult of all methods and also the most important from the strictly scientific point of view. The experimental pattern followed was pre-test, post-test, Experimental-Control Group Design.The experimental design was concerned with three kinds of variables.

Independent Variables

They were the three methods of teaching:

1. Rapprochement
2. Objective Based Teaching
3. Traditional Method of Teaching

Dependent Variables

Variables which were observed in order to determine the effects of variation in the treatment were :

1. Achievement in terms of Knowledge (K), Understanding (U), Application (A), Total Achievement (T) and Academic Attainment on science in class.

2. Creativity in terms of Fluency (F), Flexibility (X), Originality (O) and Total Creativity (C).

Concomitant Variables

These were controlled in order to see the purer effect of treatment were:

1 Memory
2 Self-Concept
3 Socio-Economic Status.

The present study involved all kinds of variables and principles of experimental design. Therefore, it was a multivariable research requiring multi-variate analysis.

Sample

The present study was confined to 90 students of both sexes of standard V of Kendriya Vidyalaya. Their age ranged between

PRE-POST EXPERIMENTAL DESIGN OF THE STUDY HAS BEEN STREAMLINED AS FOLLOWS:

	Group treatment			Length of treatment
	G1	G2	G3	
Pre-testing-Pupil -achievement	Administration of attainment test			3 days
Pre-testing Pupil creativity	Administration of relevent creativity test			3 days
Experimental Instructions treatment	Instructions 3½ based on Rapprochement	based on Objective Based Teaching	based on Traditional Method	Instructions months
Collection of data on concomitant Variables	Administration of test of -Socio-Economic Status Scale -Memory Span -Self Concept Scale			In between Treatment
Post-testing Pupil-achievement	Administration of attainment test			3 days
Post-testing pupil-creativity	Administration of creativity test			3 days
Total				4 months

9 and 11 years. They belonged to different socio-economic groups. The school was selected as the Principal agreed to offer his students for experiment, otherwise it was extremely difficult and expensive to experiment at school due to the definite instructional goals set down by the school board. In fact, it is very difficult to convince school authorities that established instructional objectives should be altered merely for the sake of testing new ideas. The task was even made more difficult by the fact there was no guarantee that the results would not be calamitious. Moreover, school authorities had to change whole time table for that particular classes. Due to these reasons it was difficult to get the stratified random sample. That is why only one school was selected where the cooperation of the principal was available and hence the sample was an incidental one. There were three sections of class V and the total

number of students were 110 but some students remained absent during the pre-tests and some had been transferred to another places and some got new admission during the experimental phase. Therefore, the present at the time of pre-testing as well as post-testing decreased to 90. There were two experimental groups and one control group.

Construction and Standardisation of Achievement Test

Measures of achievement were based on self-made tests and achievement in academic attainment in science by school test. Self made achievement test was based on the Iowa Test Battery. Keeping in view the significant features of Iowa Test Battery achievement test was constructed in the form of objective type questions, in which four possible answers were given for a single question and the student had to select the most correct answer. The same test has been used as pre-test as well as post-test. For the selection of test material text-book of science for class V was used as a guide-line.

At first 75 test items were formed and they were further analysed with respect to Knowledge (K), Understanding (U) and Application (A). Independent judgement of four experts were obtained in respect to the objectives of Knowledge, Understanding, and Application of test items, which were agreed upon by the independent judgement of majority of experts. In this ways the reliability of test items in respect to the objectives of K.U.A. was established.

Administration of the Test

Test items were standardised on the students of V standard, who were not subjects of actual experimentation. At a time, the test was administered on a group of 30 to 35 students.

Scoring of the Test

Scoring of all the achievement tests was done by appropriate procedure.

Standardisation

A statistical procedure of test standardisation and item analysis by Micheal William (1950) was applied.

Preparation of Instructional Material

Preparation of the Instructional Material for the Experimental Group II based on the rationale of Objective Based Teaching

The preparation of the instructional material for this group is based on the rationale of Objective Based Teaching (Advanced Curriculum Model of Cognitive Learning).

Taking in view a few important concepts of this curriculum model, instructional material was prepared in the form of unit plans and lesson plans. A few important terms, which are used in the preparation of plans are discussed to make the concepts more clear.

The present curriculum model consists of Expected Behavioural Outcomes (EBOs), selected and seqentially arranged content-Learning Experiences (LEs) to be provided to a learner and tools and techniques of evaluation called *Real Learning Outcomes* (RLOs).

Learning is the result of learning experiences. These learning experiences were provided by presenting the content of the prescribed book. The learning experiences are contrived by formulating instructional objectives, deriving and presenting the content in such a manner that the learner interacts with that and incorporates that for the future use. Evaluation is done in the form of RLOs side by side to attain the instructional objectives. So the model of curriculum took its shape in a chained process which consisted of (1) Instructional Objectives, (2) Content, (3) Learning Experience, (4) Evaluation. This process can be depicted as Objectives-Content-Learning Experiences-Evaluation.

The most important part in this curriculum model is that it is a totality, a gestalt, a unity and not four separate components.

The behavioural objectives need a little more explanation. Behavioural objectives involve thinking, performing muscular activities and feelings. These are respectively known as *Cognitive, Psychomotor* and *Affective Objectives*. Cognitive Objectives involve the learner in thinking process like remembering, reasoning, evaluating, judging and problem solving. Psychomotor objectives are manipulative (motor skill objectives). In this case, learner is engaged in some kind of muscular activity like playing and writing. Affective objectives are concerned with the learner's interests, feelings and attitude. Most learning includes all the three domains to some extent, often the cognitive aspects are emphasised most, but psychomotor and affective learning also play an important part. While teaching, teacher uses the techniques of probing questions or demonstrate and the students have to predict out, generalise, to formulate to hypothesis themselves. These are the cognitive objectives. But when the child is supposed to draw diagrams, it is a psychomotor behaviour. He is also supposed to admire, to enjoy or to take interest in knowing the fundamental concepts of his surrounding or environment, e.g.., How are the days and nights formed? What is water cycle? This comes under affective domain.

In the above example, the learning in all the three domains is there, yet the cognitive aspects are emphasised most.

Keeping in view this fact the instructional material was developed according to the broad objective of cognitive domain. The following four levels of objectives have been identified in this domain, which appear to form a sort of hierarchy, a graded organisation. Each level was distinguished by the nature of the mental process involved. These four levels of learning in order of complexity are as follows :

1. Knowledge (K)
2. Understanding (U)
3. Application (A)
4. Creativity (C)

1. Knowledge emphasize remembering facts, figures, symbols, letters and words. It involves following mental processes :

- recognition
- recall
- recollection
- reconstruction
- restructuring

2. Understanding emphasizes the following mental processes:

- seeing relationship
- citing examples
- discrimination
- classification
- interpretation
- verification
- generalisation among content elements.

This involves change in the thinking and imagination in the

mind of the pupil, so that he can cite, discriminate and classify rules, methods and processes. Thus in comprehension something more than remembering or reproduction is involved.

3. Application involves the ability to use information, ideas, concepts, rules, methods or processes to deal with a practical problem not encountered before. The capability of applying something require remembering and understanding of the required content, but it further involves the mental process of

- reasoning
- hypothesing
- inferring
- predicting

4. Creativity involves creations of unique proposals, plans and products. It involves the complex process of analysis, synthesis and judgement. The analysis leads to the discovery of connections and interaction between content elements, which leads to a new production (synthesis) that may be subjected to quantitative and qualitalive judgements.

On the basis of above objectives, i.e.., Knowledge, Understanding and Application the broad behavioural objectives in the context of the contents of the text book were streamlined. This is a Learner Centred Instructional Strategy for accelerating achievement through higher order-thinking. This was the first step for preparing unit/lesson plans prepared as instructional material for the experimental Group - II.

The second step in preparing lesson plan is to plan about learning experiences, Material, Methods, Modes and Media to be followed in the actual teaching of the contents. These learning experiences are contrived by the use of various combinations of stimulus modes and presentation media.

Preparation of Instructional material for the Experimental Group I (Based on the rationale of Rapprochement)

The preparation of the instructional material for this group was based on the rationale of Rapprochement. Keeping in view a few important ideas of activity based teaching of Piaget and concepts of curriculum model of behaviourism instructional material is prepared in the form of unit and lesson plans. The role of play in the cognitive development of children has been emphasised. Adaptation to the development is the essence of all intellectual functioning. A great variety of sensation and perceptual experiences can be arranged into some sort of order leading to the adaptation to the world. In fact, the whole content of the science can be arranged, in the order of adaptation. Adaptation is characterised by two important processes namely, Assimilation and Accommodation, through playful activities a child moves from the unknown into untried.

Furth (1970) says that the basic themes underlying formal science -like ordering, classifying, inferring, thinking in proposition and hypothesis are the same mental skills which make spontaneous knowledge mature, stable, logically coherent and open to new discoveries. All these basic concepts were developed through various games. Furth says that in order to put Piaget's idea in operation, let children discover the exacteogical meaning by repeated demonstration and by setting specific problems. Let children construct knowledge. It is also called *constructivism.*

The fundamental focus of Piagetian thinkers has been to stimulate development of intellect through various activities related or unrelated to the content.

Educationists and parents are still conservative in nature. They hardly realise the fact that the intellectual development is the soul aim of education at primary level, for them the traditional curriculum, syllabus and methods of teaching are highly important. Therefore, it is found that National Educational authorities framed different curriculum and have also prescribed text-books accordingly. Teachers are supposed to complete the content of text-book within the time limit prescribed by the authorities. Since the curriculum and text books are prescribed for all levels of education, the proponents of behavioural objectives had tried to classify the content according to the various levels of learning. Curriculum planners have also tried to develop the instructional material according to the behavioural objectives for all classes.

It is important to mention here that the Experimental Group II has been taught on the rationale of the same.

If that approach is adopted rigidly than Piagetian contribution is not taken care of. Nagpal (1983) felt that the aim of education according to both is the mental development only. One wants to develop it in isolation and other through text- book. Why not both be adopted simultaneously. This curiosity has encouraged to develop such a plan where both paradigms can be simultaneously used and also be culture and learner specific. Keeping this rationale in view three dimensional lesson plan was developed. The first dimension was concerned with Expected Behavioural Objectives (EBO's) as envisaged by proponents of Objective Based Teaching. In this dimension the content of the text-book was broken into various expected behavioural changes to be brought about by stimulating questions. The second dimension called *Learning Experiences* (LEs), Where various playful activities, experiments, demonstration concrete examples and related games were incorporated for the development of concepts of the text-book. Thus the developed concepts were further tested side by side by evaluating questions based on the text and local culture in terms of Real Learning Outcomes (RLOs).

In fact, it is a learner centred Instructional Strategy for accelerating attainment through higher order thinking.

Formation of Treatment Groups

To study the efficacy of three teaching-learning paradigms, three equivalent groups were formed on the ability level based on Coloured Progressive Matrices.

Administration of the Test of Intelligence

Coloured progressive Matrices (CPM) provides a practical means of assessing a person's intellectual development. It provides a valuable test for young children. Success in sets A, AB and B depends upon the apprehension of discrete figures. This adequately covers all the cognitive processes of which children under eleven years of age are capable. The three sets together provide three opportunities for a person to develop a consistent theme of thought and a scale of 36 problems as a whole is designed to assess as accurately as possible, mental development up to intellectual maturity.

The CPM was presented to students as coloured illustrations printed in a booklet which made the problem to be solved obvious with the least possible verbal explanation. There was no time limit in the given test as it was a power test. The test was conducted to make three equivalent ability groups. Scoring of this test was with the help of scoring stencil provided for the purpose. On the basis of intelligence test scores arranged in a descending order, three random groups were formed, two experimental groups (viz. Experimental Group I, Experimental Group II) and one control (C).

Actual Carrying out of the Experiment

Administration of Pre-test of Achievement

Self- made Achievement test in Science was administered on the three groups one by one as per standard procedure.

Scoring of the Test

Scoring of the test was done with respect of the 3 mental levels of cognitive learning, i.e., Knowledge (K) , Understanding (U), and Application (A).

Marks of the school test were also obtained as pre-school Achievement test.

Administration of Pre-test of Creativity

Torrance tests of creative Thinking, namely "Thinking Creativity with Words" was used. This test claim to measure fluency, flexibility and originality, through various subtasks. These test-tasks have been extensively used by research students all over the world.

Thinking Creativity with Words

This test designed by Torrance (1968). Is consisted of seven test tasks viz. Asking Questions, Guessing causes, Guessing consequences; Product Improvement; unusual use (cardboard boxes); Unusual Questions and Just Suppose. These sub-tasks claimed to measure fluency, flexibility and originality.

Rationale Underlying Sub-tasks of Verbal Creativity Test:

First three activities were named as Ask and Guess Activities. These activities were included in this battery to give subjects an opportunity to express their curiosity and give a picture of their ability to develop hypotheses and to think in terms of possibles. This concept was in harmony with the definition of creative thinking as a process. Through this activity the sensitivity toward unbroken things and toward gaps in knowledge was tested as the questions asked were those which could not be answered by merely looking at the picture. Curiosity, an important aspect of creativity was recognised as being reflected in the number and kind of questions asked. The Guess Causes and Guess Consequences activities were designed to reveal the subjects ability to formulate hypothesis concerning cause and effect. Fourth activity, i.e., Product Improvement Activity was as complex task with a high degree of face validity. To most subjects, it was an interesting task, which permitted them to "regress in the service of ego" and enabled them to play with ideas that they would not dare to express in a more serious task. The unusual uses (cardboard boxes), i.e., the fifth activity was the modification of Guilford's Brick uses test. In this activity, unusual uses were to be thought of rather than thinking of all the different things that could be put into it. Thus the task was in part a test of ability to free ones mind of a well established set. The Just Suppose activity was the last and was an adaptation of the consequences type in Guilford (1959) battery. This was designed in an attempt to elicit a higher degree of fantasy. The subject was confronted with an improbable situation and was asked to predict the possible outcomes from the introduction of a new or unbroken variable. In the present, the improbable situation to be supposed was "If clouds have strings- what will happen?". In order to respond productively to this task the subject had to play with the possibility and imagine all the things that would happen as a consequence. This kind of thinking seemed to be highly important in creative behaviour.

Administration of Creative Test

The test was given to the group comprising of 25 to 30 students. Since these tests were sensitive and the effect of instructions had been observed by researcher, therefore, the test was administered in accordance with standardised instructions. As the groups were comprised of small students, instructions were simplified, but they were the same for all students. Verbal tests, as described earlier comprised of seven sub-tasks. It was difficult for young children to sit for a long time. Therefore, first four test tasks were administered in one sitting and the remaining in the other sitting.

Scoring

For verbal tests of creativity, scoring was done with regard to fluency, flexibility and originality. Total creativity scores were also obtained by adding the scores of fluency, flexibility and originality. In this way, following components of creativity were identified. Fluency (F), Flexibility (X), Originality (O), and Total Creativity (C).

Experimental Phase

The treatment phase lasted for four months. In these four months, the total time in hours was as below :

Total school periods per week	=	12
Periods in a month	=	12 × 4
Periods for four months	=	48 approximately
	=	48 × 4
	=	192

Out of thesc 192 periods 12 periods were devoted to the data collection of Pre-Achievement-Post-Achievement Test and Pre-Creativity and Post-Creativity tests.

Hence remaining periods	=	180 periods
One period	=	40 minutes
Total time	=	180 × 40
	=	7200
	=	120 hrs.

From the above detailed analysis it is clear that 120 hours

were devoted to each group, during experimental phase. During the treatment phase, the following treatment was given.

Experimental Group I was treated on the rationale of Rapprochement. From the Chapter of Introduction, from the Instructional materials discussed in the beginning of this chapter, it is very clear that the main objective of teaching through this approach was to teach through Activity as well as the Objective Based Teaching. Keeping this motive in view, a few important ideas of Activity Based Teaching of Piaget and concepts of Curriculum Model the instructional material was prepared in the form of unit and lesson plan. In the first part content of the text-book was converted into questions based on the Expected Behavioural Outcomes (EBO's). The second part was concerned with Learning Experiences (LEs). In this way various playful activities, experiments, demonstrations, concrete examples and related games were incorporated for the developments of concepts of the text-book. And in the third part, developed concepts were further tested side by side by evaluative questions based on the text. This was termed as Real Learning Outcomes (RLO's).

Experimental Group II was taught by the instructional materials prepared on the rationale of Objective Based Teaching. In the objective based instructional material, all the lessons of the book Exploring Environment class V were converted into objective based lesson plans. The main body of the lesson plan consisted of objective based questions based on Expected Behavioural Outcomes (EBOs). Learning Experiences (LE's) were provided in the actual teaching and side by side Real Learning Outcomes (RLOs) were tested through evaluative questions.

Processing of Data

Before deciding upon the required statistical technique, nature of scores obtained on different variables considered, which were as follows:

	Type of Variables	Scale Dimension
(1)	Method of Teaching (Independent)	Nominal, i.e., Dummy Variables
(2)	Covariates (Concomitant)	Interval
(3)	Achievement Scores Creativity Scores (Dependent)	Interval

The required statistical analysis for these variables were Analysis of Variance of Kruskal Wallis test to see the effect of independent variables on the dependent variables and covariables on the dependent variables and to partial out the effect of covariables on dependent variables.

Characterisation of Key Terms and Concepts

It need hardly to mention that in any research activity, use of terms consistently with the same connotation is essential for effective communication. This is particularly important in a field of 'Education', which being a developing discipline lacks exactitude of the natural science in assigning exact meaning to the terminology it adopts in explaining theoretical models. It is, therefore, desirable to clarify some of technical terms, which to used in this study.

Treatment Variables

These were the Independent Variables, whose effect were to be studied. These are the three methods of teaching corresponding to the three groups viz.

I. Experimental Group I. It is termed as this group was

taught / treated on the rationale of Rapprochement, i.e., combination of Objective Based Teaching (OBT) and Piagetian Method of Teaching (PMT). This is hence named as Rapprochement (Rapp).

II . Experimental Group II. It is termed as this group was taught / treated with the help of Objective Based Teaching, hence named as (OBT).

III. Control Group. It is termed as it was taught / treated by the usual text and procedure, hence termed as Traditional Method of Teaching (TMT).

Dependent Variables

These are also called *Criterion Variables* or *Predictor Variables*. These were the variables on which the effect of treatments were to be observed and analysed.

Concomitant Variables

These were the Independent Variables, which indirectly or directly related to the Dependent Variables. Therefore, they are also called *Confounding Variables*. For true experimental studies, it is important to control or determine their influence. Unfortunately, it is usually very difficult to control their effect in most on-going school programmes. In such a situation, the researcher tried to determine the relationship of these variables to the other treatment and dependent variables.

4

STATISTICAL ANALYSIS OF DATA AND FINDINGS

The data has been computer processed at PC-AT-386 computer Following statistical analysis was done:

1. Central tendencies, Deviation, Skewness, Kurtosis.
2. F-test and t-test.
3. MRCA.
4. Kruskal Walis-one way analysis by ranks was computed by SPSS.

The study was a type of multivariate research in which an experimental design had been followed. More than one statistical techniques were used to examine the various hypothesis. The chapter has two parts.

Part I covers the nature of the statistical technique and their justification.

Part II deals with the findings deduced from the application of statistical techniques as per the various hypothesis.

Part I. ***Theoretical rationale of applying the various Statistics***

Before adopting any statistical technique, it is necessary to employ some rationale which enter into the choice of a statistical test.

It was essential to ascertain whether the measures of the variables are normally distributed. The results of the central tendency, SD, Skewness, Kurtosis of both pre-test and post-test scores are given in Table 4.1 (a) and (b). As each of the criterion variables had two masers, i.e., pre-test and post-test, therefore, it was decided to take the gain scores to see the comparative effect of the three treatment variables. To see the relationship among different variables both the measures, i.e., pre-and post-test scores were considered.

From the scrutiny of data in Table 4.1 (a), it is clear that total scores of pre-test are negatively stewed for knowledge, understanding and total achievement, whereas those of application, Fluency, Flexibility, Originality, Total Creativity and School Achievement are positively stewed.

TABLE - 4.1 (A)

VALUES OF CENTRAL TENDENCY, SD, SKEWNESS AND KURTOSIS OF PRE TEST SCORE OF VARIABLES

Criteria Variable	*Mean*	*Median*	*Mode*	*SD*	*Skewness*	*Kurtosis*
K	10.923	10.5	11.00	4.847	-.283	-.523
U	10.813	11.23	13.18	5.350	-.156	-.987
A	1.615	0.78	0.315	1.428	.442	-.482
T	23.352	23.5	22.88	9.509	.355	-.632
F	11.648	10.10	6.00	7.131	.368	-.497
X	2.242	1.74	1.357	1.552	.362	-.025
O	2.692	1.72	1.308	3.946	2.067	4.518
C	16.582	13.87	11.36	11.168	68.779	.540
SA	30.187	25.10	26.67	15.602	.472	-.428

(K) Knowledge, (U) Understanding, (A) Application, (T) Total Achievement, (F) Fluency, (X) Flexibility (O) Originality, (C) Creativity, (SM) School Marks

TABLE - 4.1 (b)

VALUES OF CENTRAL TENDENCY, SD, SKEWNESS AND KURTOSIS OF POST TEST SCORES OF ALL CRITERIA VARIABLES

Criteria Variable	*Mean*	*Median*	*Mode*	*SD*	*Skewness*	*Kurtosis*
K	10.923	10.16	10.72	4.726	.003	-.058
U	15.385	16.06	19.27	6.427	-.420	-.543
A	2.615	1.17	0.57	2.458	.766	-.243
T	28.923	27.60	24.00	11.653	-.172	-.189
F	16.308	15.11	15.00	9.427	.743	1.074
X	2.989	2.30	1.80	1.912	.569	.639
O	3.648	1.76	1.12	4.505	1.450	1.671
C	23.005	20.16	13.75	14.522	.786	.648
SM	41.527	33.28	26.67	20.741	.648	-.662

(K) Knowledge, (U) Understanding, (A) Application, Achievement, (A) Fluency, (F) Flexibility (X) Originality, (O) Creativity, (C) School Marks (SM).

From the security of data in Table 4.1 (a), it is clear that total scores of pre-test are negatively skewed for knowledge, understanding and total achievement, whereas those of application, Fluency, Flexibility, Originality, Total Creativity and School Markes are positively skewed. Like-wise Table 4.1 (b) shows that total scores of post-test are negatively skewed for understanding and application only and the score for Knowledge, Application, Fluency, Flexibility, Total Creativity and School Marks are positively skewed.

The first problem to be solved in analysing the data was whether to use parametric devices or non-parametric devices. According to Siegel (1955) parametric tests such as F-test and t-test are strongest or most powerful tests, as they have a variety of strong assumptions underlying their use. When a research data is analysed appropriately by a parametric test, that test will be more powerful than any other. However, the requirement is that the research data must be appropriate for the test.

However, according to other statisticians as reported by Popham (1967), this viewpoint is rejected on the ground that it confuses a measurement question with a statistical question. It is not true that the parametric analysis such as t-test cannot be computed on data, which are ordinal in nature. When the assumption constituting the statistical model for a test are in fact, not met, then the test may not be valid, i.e., a test statistic may fall in the rejection region . It is even difficult to estimate the extent to which a probability statement varies because of the inappropriate application of the test. Although some empirical evidence has been gathered to show that slight deviations in meeting the assumptions underlying parametric tests may not have radical effect on the obtained probability levels.

A number of empirical studies had demonstrated that when parametric procedures have been employed with ordinal data, they rarely distort a relationship between variables. According to Mc Nemer (1969), There exists sufficient evidence to support that marked skewness, departure from normal kurtosis and extreme differences in variance do not greatly disrupt the F-test as a basis for judging the significants in analysis of variance. The error introduced by violation of these assumptions is such that F may reach the .05 level about .06 or .07 of the time and the .01 level, which about .02 of the time. If the investigator wishes to have some assurance that he is not risking the making of type I error more often than his chosen level of judging significance, he may wish to adopt a some-what more rigorous level; requiring a computed F to reach the .01 level provides a very safe base for claiming significance at the .02 level.

But we cannot neglect the fact that non-parametric statistical tests are not systematic whereas parametric statistical tests have been systematised and different tests are simply variations on a central theme. This is true that the value of systematic approaches justifies the cost.

Since overwhelming opinion and evidence are in favour of the use of parametric technique, the same were used in the present study alongwith the non-parametric counterparts just to verify the results. Parametric techniques were preferred as they provided more flexibility for analysis. Further, a parametric procedure was more powerful, than its non-parametric counterparts. Its strength lies in the use of more available information such as deviation from the mean of the scores in the analysis, in contrast to non-parametric methods which depend on frequency counts and ranking procedures disregarding much of the information available in the data. Besides, if the sample is large, the pattern analysis will remain the same.

Keeping in view the design and complexity of the study, the following statistical of techniques are found appropriate for testing the significance of the hypotheses.

1. Analysis of variance and t-test to ascertain the relative effectiveness of treatment variables.
2. Kruskal Walis Test (X^2 cft) or analysis of variance by ranks and comparison between two groups (non-parametric device equivalent to t-test) were used for the affirmation of results arrived at by F-test and t-test.
3. Multiple Regression Correlation Analysis (MRCA) which is useful in examining simultaneously the effect of treatment variables after controlling the effect of concomitant variables. It also provides the percentage of variance accounted by various treatment and concomitant variables.

PART — II

THE RESULTS

The results below are presented as per the order of Hypothesis.

Hypothesis I

Predicts that "Significant differences exist among two experimental groups namely, Experimental Group I (Rapprochement), Experimental Group II (Objective Based Teaching) and the Control (Traditional) with respect to Achievement, School Marks and Creativity.

From the scrutiny of results, it was evident that F-value with respect to the attainment of scores in knowledge, understanding, total achievement and likewise scores of flexibility, originality, total creativity and school achievement are significant.

The scores of fluency are significant at the scores of Application in both tables are not significant. If we consider the probability level, analysis of variance shows that scores of applications are significant also at .21 level and the (Kruskal Walis) shows the significance level .59.

Results of both ANOVA's indicated that significant differences existed among the three groups and treatment had its impact on all predictor variables. As far as application is concerned though significant differences were not there at .01 or .05 level but the direction of F-ratio indicated the differences. Hence results indicate the efficacy of treatment variable.

The results of both ANOVA's were further supported by the Multiple Regression Correlation Analysis (MRCA).

TABLE - 4.2

ONE WAY ANALYSIS OF VARIANCE

Variables	Source of Variation	df	Sum of Square	MeanSquare	F-ratio	Level of Significance
K	Between Groups	2	139.5578	69.7789		
	Within groups	88	1328.3983	15.0954	4.6225	.0123
	Total	90	1467.9760			
U	Between	2	387.3396	193.6698		
	Within	88	2211.0780	25.1259	7.7080	.0008
	Total	90	2598.4176			
A	Between	2	24.6000	12.3000		
	Within	88	681.5538	7.7449	1.5881	.2101
	Total	90	706.1538			
T	Between	2	1194.6294	597.3147		
	Within	88	3545.8980	40.2943	14.8238	0000
	Total	90	4740.5275			
F	Between	2	177.6540	88.8270		
	Within	88	3091.6427	35.1323	2.5284	.0856
	Total	90	3269.2967			
X	Between	2	52.1946	26.0973		
	Within	88	350.3329	3.9811	6.5554	.0022
	Total	90	402.5275			
O	Between	2	135.4153	67.7076		
	Within	88	1136.1891	12.9112	5.2441	.0071
	Total	90	1271.6044			
C	Between	2	1026.2915	513.1457		
	Within	88	6862.4558	77.9825	6.5803	.0022
	Total	90	7888.	7473		
SA	Between	2	2563.5356	1281.7678		
	Within	88	12429.8490	141.2483	9.0746	.0003
	Total	90	14993.3846			

TABLE - 4.3

SUMMARY OF ANOVA BY RANKS & (KRUSKAL WALIS X ½ cft)

Criteria Variables	Experimental Group I N=34 Mean Rank	Experimental Group II N=30 Mean Rank	Control Group N=27 Mean Rank	X ½ cft (H values)	Level of Significance
K	55.00	45.47	35.26	8.6358	.0133
U	57.10	47.93	29.87	16.5028	.0003
A	49.57	43.70	44.06	1.0267	.5985
T	58.81	49.28	26.22	23.6972	.0000
F	49.78	51.00	35.69	5.9139	.0520
X	46.88	55.77	34.94	10.1081	.0064
O	49.16	52.37	34.94	7.2197	.0271
C	49.69	53.92	32.56	10.3807	.0056
SM	58.50	40.78	36.06	12.6279	.0018

TABLE - 4.4

VALUES OF r, R, R ½ AND R ½ CHANGE INDICATING RELATIONSHIP AND UNIQUE CONTRIBUTION OF THE THREE TREATMENT GROUP TO CRITERIA VARIABLES

Criteria Variables	Experimental Group I (Rapprochement)				Experimental Group II (Objective based teaching)				Control Group (Traditional)			
	r	R	R½	R½ch	r	R	R½	R½ch	r	R	R½	R½ch
K	.27*	.2672	0.714	.0714	-.02	.3084	.0951	.0237	-.27*	.3084	.0951	00
U	.30*	.3019	.0912	.0912	.04	.3861	.1494	.0579	-.36*	.3861	.1491	00
A	.18***	.1780	.0317	.0317	-.14	.1865	.0348	.0031	-.04	.1865	.0348	00
T	.42*	.4176	.1744	.1744	.01	.5019	.2520	.0772	-.45*	.5019	.2520	00
F	.10	.1020	.0102	.0102	.10	.2330	.0543	.0441	-.23**	.2330	.0543	00
X	.01	.0141	.0002	.0002	.31*	.3610	.1297	.1295	-.30*	.3601	.1297	00
O	.12	.1229	.0151	.0151	.19***	.3263	.1065	.0914	-32*	.3263	.1065	00
C	.13	.1265	.0160	.0160	.28**	.3607	.1301	.1141	-.36*	.3607	.1301	00
SA	.41	.4060	.1649	.15	.4135	.1710	.0061	-.27*	.4134	.1710	00	

* - .01 level of significance.

** - .05 level of significance.

*** - .10 level of significance.

The values presented revealed :

I Correlations of Experimental Group I was positive and

significant at .01 level to Knowledge, Understanding. Achievement, and School Marks and at .05 level to application.

II .Correlation of Experimental Group II was positive and significant at .01 level to Flexibility and Originality, and Creativity.

III The relationship of the control group to all criteria variable was negatively significant Knowledge , Understanding, Total Achievement, Flexibility , Originality , Creativity, and School Achievement and Fluency.

The treatment variable was introduced in the Hierarchial analytical procedure to MRCA as per the magnitude of their relationship to criteria variables, which varied from significant positive, moderate and significant negative for Experimental Group I (Rapprochement), Experiment Group II (Objective Based Teaching) and Control (Traditional) respectively.

Since the Experimental Group I entered first in hierarchy due to its high 'r', the value of 'R' were same as 'r' where-as in case of Experimental Group II and the control the values of 'R' are different than their corresponding 'r' values. It was due to the multiple effect of Experimental Group I on their R.

Further the values of R for Experimental Group II and of the control group remained the same. It was due to the negative relationship of the control group with all criteria variables and it could not add anything to the R of Experimental group II and hence same 'R' value was carried on for the control group too. Since the values of R for both groups remained same and hence there was no effect on the corresponding values of R^2 and R^2 change of the control group.

R^2 indicated the percentage of variance explained by these treatment variables on criteria variables. R^2 for Experimental Group

II (Objective Based Teaching) included the percentage contribution of Experimental Group I (Rapproachment). Therefore, its quantum of R^2 is more than that of Experimental Group I. But the 'R' change indicates the unique contribution (variance) of each variable with respect to all criteria variables. The different values in the column of 'R^2 change' revealed that there existed differences in the three groups. The percentage contribution of the control group was zero and comparative values of Experimental Group I and Experimental Group II for various predictor variables are in Table 4.5.

TABLE - 4.5

VALUES OF PERCENTAGE OF CONTRIBUTION EXPLAINED BY THREE TREATMENT GROUP WITH RESPECT TO TAL CRITERIA VARIABLES

Criteria Variables	Contribution of Experimental Group I	Contribution of Experimental Group II	Contribution of Control Group
K	7.14%	2.37%	00
V	9.12%	5.79%	00
A	3.17%	0.31%	00
T	17.44%	7.72%	00
F	1.02%	4.41%	00
X	0.02%	12.95%	00
O	1.51%	9.14%	00
C	1.60%	11.41%	00
SA	16.49%	0.61%	00

All these above discussed results lead to the conclusion that significant differences existed among three groups with respect to, the all criteria variables. The rapprochement is an effective technique in classroom teaching and it has positive impact on academic attainment. The ACMCL as an instructional strategy nurture the creative potential. Hence, it is proved that both are Learner Centered Instructional Strategies accelerating academic altainment through higher order thinking.

Hypothesis II

States that - "Children taught by Rapprochement show higher scores on Achievement in terms of Knowledge (K), Understanding (U), Application (A), Achievement (A), School Achievement (SA), and Creativity in terms of Fluency (F), Flexibility (X), Originality (O) and Creativity (C) than those taught by the traditional method".

The result of both ANOVA's indicated that significant differences existed among three treatment groups. Further, it was essential to ascertain their intergroup differences. For that purpose various t-tests were conducted. Besides t-test, multiple comparisons between groups (Non-parametric) were also done. The results of t-test and multiple comparison between groups to test the above hypothesis was done.

All the t-values were significant except application (A). From the scrutiny of Table 5.4, it is obvious that t-values are significant at .01 level for Knowledge, Understanding, Achievement, Originality, Creativity, School Achievement and significant at .10 level for Fluency and Flexibility but non-F significant for application. Yet the direction indicated impact on it also.

The findings were further confirmed by the results obtained through multiple comparison between Groups. The results had shown that Mean Rank differences were significant at .01 level for Understanding, Achievement and significant for Knowledge and Creativity. The Mean Rank differences for Application, Fluency , Flexibility and Originality were though non-significant yet indicated the direction of its impact.

TABLE - 4.6

t VALUES SHOWING SIGNIFICANT DIFFERENCES BETWEEN THE MEANS OF EXPERIMENTAL GROUP I (RAPPROCHEMENT) AND CONTROL GROUP (TRADITIONAL) ON ACHIEVEMENT IN TERMS OF KNOWLEDGE (K), UNDERSTANDING (U), APPLICATION (A), TOTAL ACHIEVEMENT (T), CREATIVITY IN TERMS OF FLUENCY (F), FLEXIBILITY (X), ORIGINALITY (O), CREATIVITY (C) AND SCHOOL ACHIEVEMENT (SA).

Criteria Variables	Experimental Group II Mean (M_1)	Control Group III Mean (M3)	Mean Difference	t-Value
K	1.412	-1.630	3.0425	1.7085-.10
				2.048-.05
				2.7068-.01
U	6.529	1.481	5.048	2.7695-.10
			3.320	-.05
				4.3879-.01
A	1.412	.593	.819	1.1904-.10
				1.4270-.05
			1.8860	-.01
T	9.353	.444	8.909	2.7152-.10
				3.255-.05
			4.3019	-.01
F	5.412	2.481	2.931	2.5353-.10
			3.039	-.05
			4.0168	-.01
X	.794	-.148	.942	.8535-.10
			1.023	-.05
			1.3522	-.01
O	1.529	-.926		1.5370-.10
			2.4551	.84-.05
				2.435-.01
C	8.029	1.407	6.62	23.777-.10
				4.528-.05
				5.9846-.01
SA	18.441	6.333	12.109	5.8375-.10
				6.0944-.05
				8.0544-.01

TABLE - 4.7

MULTIPLE COMPARISON BETWEEN GROUPS SHOWING SIGNIFICANT DIFFERENCES BETWEEN THE MEAN RANKS OF EXPERIMENTAL GROUP I (RAPPROCHEMENT) AND CONTROL GROUP (TRADITIONAL) ON ACHIEVEMENT IN TERMS OF KNOWLEDGE (K), UNDERSTANDING (U), APPLICATION (A), ACHIEVEMENT (T), CREATIVITY IN TERMS OF FLUENCY (F), FLEXIBILITY (X), ORIGINALITY (O), CREATIVITY (T) AND SCHOOL ACHIEVEMENT (SA).

Criteria Variables	Experimental Group II Mean Rank (R_1)	Experimental Group III Mean Rank (R_3)	Mean Rank Difference
K	55.00	35.26	19.74
U	57.10	29.87	27.23
A	49.57	44.06	5.51
T	58.81	26.22	32.59
F	49.78	35.69	14.09
X	46.88	34.04	12.84
O	49.16	34.94	14.22
C	49.69	32.56	17.13
SA	58.50	36.06	22.44

Critical Difference	-	Level of Significance
14.48	-	.10
16.29	-	.05
20.078	-	.01

On the basis of all statistical results, it is concluded that Rapprochement as a teaching strategy is effective in the development of intellect in terms of academic attainment and creativity. It is indeed a Learner Centered Strategy accelerating higher order thinking.

Hypothesis III

Predicts that "Children taught by Objective Based Teaching show higher scores on Achievement in terms of Knowledge, Understanding, Application, Total Achievement, School Achievement and Creativity in terms of Fluency, Flexibility, Originality and Creativity than taught by the Traditional Method".

TABLE - 4.8

t VALUES SHOWING SIGNIFICANT DIFFERENCES BETWEEN THE MEANS OF EXPERIMENTAL GROUP II (OBJECTIVE BASED TEACHING) AND CONTROL GROUP (TRADITIONAL ON ACHIEVEMENT IN TERMS OF KNOWLEDGE , UNDERSTANDING, APPLICATION, ACHIEVEMENT, CREATIVITY IN TERMS OF FLUENCY, FLEXIBILITY, ORIGINALITY, TOTAL CREATIVITY AND SCHOOL ACHIEVEMENT

Criteria Variables	Experimental Group II Mean (M_2)	Control Group III Mean (M_3)	Mean Difference	Critical Difference
K	-.067	-1.630	1.697	1.757-.10
				2.1075-.05
				2.7852-.01
U	4.733	1.481	3.252	2.206-.10
				2.645-.05
				3.495-.01
A	.200	593	.393	1.2247-.10
				1.468-.05
				1.9404-.01
T	5.533	.444	5.089	2.7939-.10
				3.349-.05
				4.979-.01
F	5.667	2.481	3.186	2.6088-.10
				3.1274-.05
				4.133-.01
X	1.767	-.148	1.915	.0878-.10
				1.0527-.05
				1.3913-.01
O	1.933	-.926	2.559	1.5815-.10
				1.8959-.05
				2.5056-.01
C	9.367	1.407	7.96	3.8867-.10
				4.6594-.05
				6.1579-.01
SA	8.867	6.333	2.534	5.2307-.10
				6.270-.05
				8.2871-.01

TABLE - 4.9

MULTIPLE COMPARISON BETWEEN GROUP SHOWING SIGNIFICANT DIFFERENCES BETWEEN THE MEAN RANKS OF EXPERIMENTAL GROUP II (OBJECTIVE BASED TEACHING) AND CONTROL GROUP (TRADITIONAL) ON ACHIEVEMENT IN SCIENCE IN TERMS OF KNOWLEDGE, UNDERSTANDING, APPLICATION , ACHIEVEMENT, CREATIVITY IN TERMS OF FLUENCY, FLEXIBILITY, ORIGINALITY, TOTAL CREATIVITY AND SCHOOL ACHIEVEMENT

Criteria Variables	Experimental Group II Mean Rank (R_2)	Control Group III Mean Rank (R_3)	Mean Rank Difference
K	45.47	35.26	10.21
U	47.93	29.87	18.06
A	43.70	44.06	-.36
T	49.28	26.22	23.06
F	51.00	35.69	15.31
X	55.77	34.04	21.73
O	52.37	34.94	17.43
C	53.92	32.96	21.36
SM	40.78	36.06	4.72

Critical difference	-	level of significance
14.902	-	.10
16.766	-	.05
20.659	-	.01

From the results, it was evident that t-values were significant at .01 level for Achievement and Flexibility and Creativity and significant for Understanding , Fluency , Originality and non-significant for Knowledge, Application and School Marks.

The results had indicated that Mean Rank differences between the 2 groups were significant for Total Achievement and significant at for Understanding, Flexibility, Originality, Creativity, and significant for Fluency.

They are non-significant for Knowledge Application and School Marks, but the direction indicated the superiority of ACMCL in these also.

All the above results clearly suggested that Objective Based Teaching is better than the Traditional Method of Teaching.

TABLE - 4.10

t-VALUES SHOWING SIGNIFICANT DIFFERENCES BETWEEN THE MEANS OF EXPERIMENTAL GROUP I (RAPPROCHEMENT) AND EXPERIMENTAL GROUP II (OBJECTIVE BASED TEACHING) ON ACHIEVEMENT IN TERMS OF KNOWLEDGE, UNDERSTANDING, APPLICATION, ACHIEVEMENT AND CREATIVITY IN TERMS OF FLUENCY, FLEXIBILITY, ORIGINALITY, CREATIVITY AND SCHOOL ACHIEVEMENT

Criteria Variables	Experimental Group I Mean (M_1)	Experimental Group II Mean (M_2)	Mean Difference	Critical Difference
K	1.412	-.067	1.479 1.345	1.6149-.10 1.9360-.05 2.5586-.01
U	6.529	4.733	1.796	2.083-.10 2.497-.05 3.330-.01
A	1.412	.200	1.212	1.154-.10 1.386-.05 3.3255-.01
T	9.353	5.533	.969	2.6377-.10 3.16-.05 4.179-.01
F	5.412	5.667	.255	2.4637-.10 2.953-.05 3.9034-.01
X	.794	1.767	.96	.8293-.10 .9942-.05 1.3139-.01
O	1.529	1.933	.404	1.4935-.10 1.7905-.05 2.3662-.01
C	8.029	9.367	1.338	3.6706-.10 4.4003-.05 5.8155-.01
SA	18.441	8.867	9.574	4.9399-.10 5.922-.05 7.8266-.01

Hypothesis IV

Predicts that "Children taught by Rapprochement show higher scores on Achievement in terms of Knowledge, Understanding, Application, Achievement, School Achievement and Creativity in terms of Fluency, Flexibility, Originality and Total Creativity than taught by Objective Based Teaching".

t-test were calculated to ascertain the validity of this hypothesis, Multiple comparison between groups too was done to verify the validity of the results.

TABLE - 4.11

MULTIPLE COMPARISON BETWEEN GROUPS SHOWING SIGNIFICANT DIFFERENCES BETWEEN THE MEAN RANKS OF EXPERIMENTAL GROUP I (RAPPROCHEMENT) AND EXPERIMENTAL GROUP II (OBJECTIVE BASED TEACHING) ON ACHIEVEMENT IN TERMS OF KNOWLEDGE, UNDERSTANDING, APPLICATION, TOTAL ACHIEVEMENT AND CREATIVITY IN TERMS OF FLUENCY, FLEXIBILITY, ORIGINALITY, TOTAL CREATIVITY AND SCHOOL ACHIEVEMENTS

Criteria Variables	Experimental Group II Mean Rank (R_1)	Experimental Group II Mean Rank (R_2)	Mean Difference
K	55.00	45.47	9.53
U	57.10	47.93	9.17
A	49.57	43.70	5.87
T	58.81	49.28	9.53
F	49.78	51.00	-1.22
X	46.88	55.77	-8.89
O	49.16	52.37	-3.21
C	49.69	53.92	-4.23
SM	58.50	40.78	17.72

Critical Difference	-	Level of Significance
14.074	-	.10
15.834	-	.05
19.51	-	.01

The scrutiny of t-values is the superiority of Rapprochement in the development of Flexibility (X) and School Achievement (SA) in comparison to Objective Based Teaching.

Though no significant differences were observed with respect to Knowledge, Understanding, Application, Achievement, Fluency, Originality and Creativity.

Further, the results clearly indicated that values of mean rank differences were significant for School Achievement. They were non- significant for Knowledge, Understanding, Application, Achievement, Fluency, Originality and Creativity.

As far as the obtained mean scores are concerned, the mean scores of Experimental Group I for Knowledge, Understanding, Application, Achievement are more, i.e., 1.412, 6.529, 1.412 and 9.353 respectively than the mean scores of Experimental Group II which were -.067, 4.733, .200 and 5.5331 respectively for the same variables. Thus the mean scores of Experimental Group I were higher than those of Experimental Group II. In the case of Fluency, Flexibility, Originality, Creativity, the Obtained mean scores were higher in Experimental Group II, i.e., 5.667, 1.767, 1.933, 9.367 respectively than those of Experimental Group I which were 5.412, .794, 1.529 and 8.029 respectively.

This was verified again with the results which had indicated that the mean rank scores were higher again for Knowledge, Understanding, Application, Total Achievement for Experimental Group I, i.e., 55, 57.10, 49.57 and 58.81 than the scores of Experimental Group II which were 45.47, 47.93, 43.70 and 49.28. But mean rank scores of Fluency, Flexibility, Originality, Creativity were higher for Experimental Group II, they were 51.00, 55.77, 52.37, and 53.92 and the mean scores for the same variables for Experimental Group I were 49.78, 46.88, 49.16 and 49.69, which were less than those of Experimental Group II.

The trend of superiority in Experimental Group I to Experimental Group II for Knowledge, Understanding, Application, Total Achievement in visible but regarding Fluency, Flexibility, Originality, Total Creativity trend shows the superiority of Experimental Group II over Experimental Group I.

The observations to MRCA also made it clear that the Experimental Group I explained more variance, i.e., 7.14 per cent, 9.12 per cent 3.17 per cent and 17.44 per cent for Knowledge, Understanding, Application and Achievement, than that explained by Experimental Group II which explained 2.37 per cent, 5.79 per cent, 0.31 per cent and 7.72 per cent respectively. Further, the results of Fluency, Flexibility, Originality, Creativity made it evident the Experimental Groups II explained more variance for those variables viz. 4.41per cent, 12.95 per cent 9.14 per cent and 11.41per cent that these of 01.02 per cent, 0.02 per cent, 1.51per cent and 1.60 per cent of Experimental Group I. It should be very clear that the mean scores or mean rank scores had shown this trend but they were not significant.

Thus the data supported hypothesis in respect to the School Achievement only, i.e., children taught by Rapprochement show higher scores only on School Achievement than taught by the Objective Based Teaching though the trend was favourable for Knowledge, Understanding, Application and Total Achievement for the same group. But the trend was favourable for experimental Group II for Fluency, Flexibility, Originality and Creativity.

In nut shell, it is safe to conclude that Rapprochement is a effective technique for Academic Achievement and Objective Based Teaching is an effective measure for the development of creativity.

Hypothesis V

Predicts that "There is no relationship of creativity

components, i.e., Fluency, Flexibility, Originality, Creativity to the levels of Achievements, i.e., Knowledge, Understanding, Application, Achievement (A) and School Marks ".

To test this hypothesis correlation coefficients were computed. The results:

TABLE - 4.12

INDICES OF CORRELATIONS OF CREATIVITY IN TERMS OF FLUENCY (F), FLEXIBILITY (X), ORIGINALITY (O), TOTAL CREATIVITY (C), AND ACHIEVEMENT IN TERMS OF KNOWLEDGE (K), UNDERSTANDING (U), APPLICATION (A), TOTAL ACHIEVEMENT (T) AND SCHOOL ACHIEVEMENT (SA) FOR PRE-AND POST-TEST SCORE

	Pre-Test Score					Post -Test Score				
	K	U	A	T	SA	K	U	A	T	SM
F	.43*	.39*	.43*	.50*	.47*	.53*	.48*	.55*	.60*	.53*
X	.25**	.32*	.33*	.36*	.43*	.47*	.49*	.53*	.57*	.49*
O	.26*	.38*	.20**	.38*	.44*	.47*	.47*	.64*	.59*	.54*
C	.26*	.43*	.39*	.50*	.51*	.57*	.53*	.68*	.66*	.59*

* .01 Level of Significance.

** .05 Level of Significance.

This revealed that measures of school achievement were related significantly to all creativity components. Hence due to the positive relationship of creativity and achievement the hypothesis was rejected.

Hypothesis VI

States that "There was no relationship of Creativity Components, i.e. Fluency, Flexibility, Originality and Creativity to Memory".

TABLE - 4.13

INDICES OF CORRELATIONS OF MEMORY AND CREATIVITY COMPONENTS, i.e., FLUENCY (F), FLEXIBILITY (X), ORIGINALITY (O), TOTAL CREATIVITY (C) FOR PRE-AND POST-TEST SCORES

Pre-Test Score					Post-Test Score			
	F	X	O	C	F	X	O	C
MEMORY	.34*	.21**	.23*	.32*	.31*	.19***	.29**	.32

* 0.01 Level of Significance.

** 0.05 Level of Significance.

*** 0.01 Level of Significance.

The figures in the above table reveals that memory is related to all components of creativity. Therefore, the hypothesis 6 is rejected.

Hypothesis VII

Predicts that "There is no relationship of Creativity Components, i.e., Fluency, Flexibility, Originality, and Creativity to Self-Concept".

TABLE - 4.14

INDICES OF CORRELATIONS OF SELF-CONCEPT AND CREATIVE COMPONENTS, i.e., FLUENCY, FLEXIB-LITY , ORIGINALITY, CREATIVITY FOR PRE-AND POST TEST SCORES

Pre Test Score					Post Test Score			
	F	X	O	C	F	X	O	C
Self-concept	.43*	.40*	.29*	.43*	.40*	.46*	.44*	.46*

* 0.01 Level of Significance.

Table 4.14 shows that self-concept is related to all components, of Creativity, On the basis of above findings null hypothesis No. 7 is rejected.

TABLE - 4.15

INDICES OF CORRELATIONS OF SES AND CREATIVITY COMPONENTS, i.e., FLUENCY, FLEXIBILITY , ORIGINALITY , CREATIVITY FOR PRE-AND POST TEST-SCORES.

Pre-Test Score					Post -Test Score			
	F	X	O	C	F	X	O	C
SES	.27*	18***	.28	.30*	.22**	.22**	.30*	.27*

* 0.01 Level of Significance.

** 0.05 Level of Significance.

Table 4.15 shows that socio economic status is significantly related to all components of creativity. Hence hypothesis . 8 is rejected.

Hypothesis IX

Predicts that "There is no relationship of Creativity Components, i.e., Fluency, Flexibility, Originality, and Creativity to Intelligence".

TABLE - 4.16

INDICES OF CORRELATION OF INTELLIGENCE TO CREATIVITY COMPONENTS, i.e., FLUENCY, FLEXIBILITY, ORIGINALITY , CREATIVITY FOR PRE-AND POST TEST SCORES.

Pre-Test Score					Post Test Score			
	F	X	O	C	F	X	O	C
Intelligence	.37*	.32*	.46*	.44*	.25**	.24**	.25**	.29*

* 0.01 Level of Significance.

** 0.05 Level of Significance.

Results of Table 4.16 reveals that intelligence is significantly related to creativity components. Therefore, the null hypothesis 9 is rejected.

Hypothesis X

States that "There is no relationship of levels of Achievement, i.e., Knowledge, Understanding, Application, Achievement and School Achievement to Memory".

TABLE - 4.17

INDICES OF CORRELATIONS OF MEMORY TO THE LEVELS OF ACHIEVEMENT, i.e., KNOWLEDGE, UNDERSTANDING, APPLICATION , ACHIEVEMENT FOR PRE AND POST TEST SCORES

Pre-Test Score						Post Test Score				
	K	U	A	T	SA	K	U	A	T	SA
Memory	.42*	.24**	.32*	.39*	.32*	.44*	.42*	.42*	.50*	.47*

* 0.01 Level of Significance.

** 0.05 Level of Significance.

The results in Table 4.17 indicate that memory is significantly related with achievement measures. Hence, the null hypothesis 10 is rejected.

Hypothesis XI

Predicts that "There is no relationship of levels of Achievement, i.e., Knowledge, Understanding, Application and School Achievement to Self-Concept".

To test this hypothesis correlation coefficient are computed. The relevant data are presented in Table 4.18.

Table 4.18 shows that self-concept is significantly related to all the measures of achievement. Hence, the null hypothesis 11 is rejected.

Hypothesis XII

States that "There is no relationship of levels of Achievement, i.e., Knowledge, Understanding, Application and School to Socio-Economic Status".

TABLE - 4.18

INDICES OF CORRELATION OF SELF-CONCEPT TO THE LEVELS OF ACHIEVEMENT, i.e., KNOWLEDGE, UNDERSTANDING, APPLICATION, ACHIEVEMENT FOR PRE-AND POST -TEST SCORES

	Pre-Test Score					Post Test Score				
	K	U	A	T	A	K	U	A	T	SA
Self-concept	.54*	.34*	.35*	.51*	.47*	.42*	.43*	.49*	.51*	.50

* 0.01 Level of Significance.

TABLE - 4.19

INDICES SHOWING CORRELATIONS OF SES TO THE LEVELS OF ACHIEVEMENT, i.e., KNOWLEDGE, UNDERSTANDING, APPLICATION, ACHIEVEMENT FOR PRE -AND POST -TEST SCORES

	Pre Test Score					Post Test Score				
	K	U	A	T	SA	K	U	A	T	SA
SES	.20**	.20**	.15	.24**	33**	.36**	.35*	.35*	.41*	.45*

* 0.01 Level of Significance.

** 0.01 Level of Significance.

Results of Table 4.19 shows that socio-economic status is significantly related to all the measures of achievement. On the basis of above findings null hypothesis 12 is rejected.

Hypothesis XIII

Predicts that "There is no relationship of levels of Achievement, i.e., Knowledge (K), Understanding (U), Application (A), Total Achievement (T) and School Achievement (SA) to Intelligence".

Table 4.20 shows that intelligence is related to all the measures of achievement. Hence, null hypothesis 13 is rejected.

TABLE - 4.20

INDICES SHOWING CORRELATIONS OF INTELLIGENCE TO THE LEVEL OF ACHIEVEMENT, i.e., KNOWLEDGE (K), UNDERSTANDING (U), APPLICATION (A), TOTAL ACHIEVEMENT (T) FOR PRE-AND POST -TEST SCORES

Pre-Test Score						Post Test Score				
	K	U	A	T	SA	K	U	A	T	SA
Intelligence	.46*	.38*	.37*	.50*	.45*	.43*	.42*	.52*	.51*	.48*

* 0.01 Level of Significance.

Hypothesis XIV

States that "There is no relationship among Memory, Self Concept, Socio-Economic Status and Intelligence".

a. Self-concept and Memory.

b. Self-concept and Socio-Economic Status.

c. Self-concept and Intelligence.

d. Memory and Socio-economic Status.

e. Memory and Intelligence.

f. Socio-Economic Status and Intelligence.

To test this hypothesis coefficient of correlations are computed which are given in Table 4.21.

TABLE - 4.21

INDICES SHOWING CORRELATIONS OF SELF-CONCEPT MEMORY, SOCIO-ECONOMIC STATUS AND INTELLIGENCE

	SC	M	SES	IT
SC	-	.29*	.25*	.39*
M	-	-	.27*	.47*
SES	-	-	-	.27*

* .01 Level of Significance

The table reveals that self-concept is significantly related to memory, socio-economic status and intelligence. Memory is significantly related to socio-economic Status. Again socio-economic status is related to Intelligence. Hence hypothesis 14 is rejected.

5

DISCUSSIONS AND CONCLUSIONS OF RESULTS

Discussion of Results Regarding the Comparative Effect of Methods of Teaching

The primary purpose of the investigation was to study the relative effect of Rapprochement, Objective Based Teaching and Traditional Method of Teaching on achievement. On the basis of results presented the conclusions arrived at are as follows :

Significant differences exist among three groups namely Experimental Group I (Rapprochement), Experimental Group II (Objective Based Teaching) and the Control (Traditional) with respect to their impact on Achievement and Creativity.

The data on mean scores of the different teaching methods and the results of the two types of Analysis of variance of the scores on three teaching methods clearly suggested that the three methods viz. Rapprochement, Objective Based Teaching and Traditional differ significantly from one another in.

Scores of achievement and creativity Again, the results of MRCA shown indicated that the three groups differ with reference to their percentage contribution to different criteria variables. They also have indicated the superiority of rapprochement. The Experimental Group I was provided with the instructional material based on the rationale of rapprochement - a combination of Objective Based Teaching and Piagetian Method of Teaching. Objective Based Teaching is concerned with the objective based instructional and evaluation materials. It is a three dimensional paradigm, i.e., objectives (EBO's). Instructions (LEs) and Evaluation (RLO's) Piagetians believe in the development of thinking process through various playful activities and concrete examples and experiences. This concept of Piagetian thinking was incorporated at the second level, i.e., Instructions. In this way, objectives were planned in terms of EBO's in relation to the content and to achieve these EBO's, activities and concrete experiences were incorporated. The pure verbal question-answer discussion was generally avoided. These concrete playful experiences helped in stimulating question-answer session. The developed concepts were further evaluated through appropriate techniques, i.e., Real Learning Outcomes (RLO's).

Thus the approach seemed to be logical and scientific as it gives equal emphasis to each and every aspect of the teaching-learning process. It emphasises the input, the process and the output. Not only this, this approach provides ample opportunities to the learner in the form of related and identical tasks to the school curriculum. These tasks in turn enhance the thinking process of the learner, on which all type of learning is grounded.

Experimental Group II was treated on the rationale of Objective Based Teaching. In this approach, there was a relationship between subject matter, mental process and behaviour, as it is assumed that specific behaviours and specific mental processes signify the level of intellectual development. The main objective of teaching according to this approach is to stimulate cognitive developmental process verbally, which gets reflected in the verbal behaviour of the learner. In other words, in the processes of teaching learning the changed behaviour of the learner in the form of responses give evidence for making inferences regarding the development of the intellect. It is with this precise goal in view that the appropriate learning experiences in the form of verbal questions from the prescribed text-book were provided for the development of concepts. Functionally, it means that the content of the text-book was used to stimulate mental processes and were therefore evaluated with reference to the same.

The control group was taught with the traditional method. It is the method being followed in our schools, primarily as the "pouring in " of facts. The teacher and the child follow the prescribed syllabus rigidly without any freedom. The child is supposed to be a good receiver of the given knowledge. In this method more emphasis is given to memory testing wherein the real purpose of education (i.e., cognitive development) remains suppressed.

The above discussion of these methods reveals that they are basically different. The results reported in empirically supported the same. Thus, it can be concluded that in one method (Rapprochement), emphasis is given to cognitive development through preplanned objective based instructional and evaluation material, while giving due importance to a variety of concrete tasks which are related to his/her thinking process. In the Objective Based Teaching, the target is achieved by making the text as a medium. In the traditional method cognitive development is not properly taken care of. The emphasis is generally on passing on information. Therefore, the obtained results are logically plausible. The arrived results are in harmony with the suggestion as referred by Lunzer (1976), Nagpal (1983), Mahendra (1986) and Yadav (1989).

II Children taught by Rapprochement show higher scores on achievements.

The findings show that pupils taught by Rapprochement achieved higher mean score in respect of all the dependent variables than pupils taught by the traditional method. The mean performance of the group taught by Rapprochement method differ significantly.

The results of the study proved that the instructional material prepared and the method selected with reference to the mental processes helped in the development of higher learning levels. Examination of the t-values, sum of ranks in X ½ cft and R^2 change value of MRCA with regard to all dependent variables clearly confirmed the genuine effect of Rapprochement. The conclusions are theoretically justified. The theoretical superiority of this has been realised by Lunzer (1976), Nagpal (1983), Yadav (1989) and Mahendra (1986).

The superiority of Rapprochement, over the traditional method is perhaps due to more flexibility and involvement of concrete experience in teaching - learning process. Due to better classroom interaction, there is less probability of losing interest, questions relating to diffent levels of cognitive development and presentation of concrete examples and activities helped in the development of intellect through attainment of the concepts. Moreover the immediate feedback of their learning behaviour through questions relating to Real Learning Outcomes also helped in higher acquisition of content. In the traditional method, on the contrary, there is hardly any stimulation and interaction for any activity. Teachers generally follow the lecture method ; wherein the teaching - learning process is generally passive, consequently there is less likelihood of development of thinking among children. Hence obtained results are logically sound.

Rapprochement has been again proved better than that to traditional even for the development of creativity. Rapprochement is a practical and creative approach to teaching. Thus, there is a direct effect of this technique of teaching on the development of creativity. Students are not able to develop it through conventional method. This is so because they are not allowed to make use of their creative thinking abilities, which are inherent and innate to some degree in everybody.

Anderson (1964), Kirkpatrick (1964), Ebel (1969), Khire (1977) and Lefrencois (1972) have rightly summed up the current educational system, the methods of teaching and the teacher as a rigid, rule bound and authoritarian with intellectually dull classroom environment.

Rapprochement, on the other hand, provides concrete experiences and activities related to the concepts to the students, so as to provoke their mental abilities. Thus, it can appropriately be said that this method of teaching is a mode of creative development. Beside these, maximum opportunities were provided to the students for an effective expression of their ideas and feeling. Therefore , the obtained results are logically plausible.

III The children taught by Objective Based Teaching show higher scores on Achievement and Creativity than taught by the Traditional Method.

The results show that pupil taught by the Objective Based Teaching method Achievement scored higher in Achievement, than pupils taught by the traditional method. The mean performance of both groups differ significantly. The obtained raw-score also indicated the superiority of this method.

The results shown indicated the same pattern of results. The results of this study are in consonance with the findings of Dave (1976), Pritam Singh (1978), Manjula (1980), Nagpal (1983), Vanita (1985) and Mahendra (1986).

The superiority of the Objective Based Teaching over that of the Traditional was perhaps due to more discussion and better classroom interaction in Objective Based Teaching. Objective based instructional and evaluation material used in the form of question-answer technique, helped in the development of intellect through attainment of concepts. Whereas in traditional method no such stimulation was generally given to the children and they remained passive listeners.

Objective Based Teaching has been proved better in the development of creativity than the traditional method. The better classroom interaction, stimulated the students to think divergently and obviously helped in nurturing their higher mental abilities. Hence, the obtained results are logically sound .

IV The children taught by Rapprochement show higher scores on Achievement and Creativity than taught by Objective Based Teaching.

The data show that pupils taught by Rapprochement achieved higher mean scores in School Marks than pupils taught by the Objective Based Teaching. The mean performance of the two groups differed significantly for School Achievement.

Further data has shown that pupils taught by Objective Based Teaching had higher mean scores on Creativity than pupils taught by Rapprochement.

From the above results following conclusions are drawn:

The children taught by Rapprochement had show higher acquisition on School Marks (SM) than taught by the OBT. The children taught by OBT scored higher on Creativity (C) than taught by Rapprochement. Several explanation are possible.

In teaching based on Rapprochement, the global development

of intellectual capacities are emphasised, in the context of preplanned Objective Based Teaching, due importance is given to the concrete examples and experiments. These are the part and parcel of a teaching-learning process which are related with the classroom situation and content of the text. Hence, they helped in the development of concepts.

It indicates that the verbal discussion and question - answer session stimulated the student's mental process thus developing their higher order thinking.

Statistically, the results had proved that both the approaches are superior to the traditional one, but in comparison to each other they are equally effective. A number of empirical studies by Owen (1973), Bingham Newman (1975), Lavatelle's (1976), Weikart (1973), PPEP (1947), Kami (1974), Nagpal (1983) had proved that Piagetian approach is not very much relevant to the school learning in Indian setup hence, did not prove much effective. The results of the study had proved that if the Piagetian thinking can be incorporated with school learning than no doubt it can be as effective as the other existing instructional strategies like that of Objective Based Teaching.

Creativity and Achievement

There is a relationship of Creativity Components, to School achievement.

Results presented revealed :

(a) Fluency is significantly related to knowledge understanding, application, and school marks.

b) Flexibility is significantly related to knowledge, understanding, application and school marks.

c) Originality is significantly related to the knowledge, understanding, application and school marks.

The overall results indicated the strong association between content and objectives of achievement, with that of the components of creativity on standardised tests of creativity. The results are logically sound. Several explanations are given for this.

Objectives (knowledge, understanding, application of achievement are directly related with the content which are further part and parcel of mental processes, indicating cognitive development. It means any piece of content has a hierarchy of mental process, referring the level of the development of intellect which are also measured through standardised creativity tests. It means the mental abilities developed through instructional strategies having content of prescribed syllabus are tested through two different measures, i.e., achievement test and standardised creativity test. Both are related with the developed intellect and hence are positively related.

There is another way of looking at the results. Levels of achievement and creativity components as indicated by research studies of Dave (1976), Pritam Singh (1978) and Nagpal (1983) are hierarchically related and cumulative, in nature. The analysis of data revealed consistent and systematic increase in the relationship of creativity components to that of achievement levels.

Components of creativity are hierarchically related with the achievement. The lower component of creativity, i.e., Fluency is highly associated with the achievement and this relationship gradually decreases with the higher component of creativity, i.e., (with flexibility and originality) and achievement.

The safest conclusion to be drawn from this is that the achievement tests being speed tests requires more ideas in a limited period so fluency is highly related. The higher levels of creativity like flexibility and oringniality take time for their development. For this, relaxed environment is required, which is not available in the test situation. Hence, relationship of Flexibility and originality with achievement is affected adversely.

The results can be interpreted horizontally as well as vertically. From both directions the consistent change is visible.

Horizontally the relationship of creativity components and levels of learning may be interpreted as.

Fluency is the lowest component of creativity. Its correlation to the levels of learning and achievement ranged from .43 to .50 in pre-test scores and .53 to .60) in post-test scores. Originality is the third highest component and the range of its relationship to the levels of learning and achievement ranged from .26 to .38 in pre-test scores and .47 to .59 in post-test scores.

Interpretation of results through vertical direction revealed that knowledge has significant relationship with all creativity measures. The relationship of understanding is more with the components of creativity. There is further increase in the relationship of application to the creativity components respectively for F, X, O and C. This clearly indicates the complexity of the hierarchy of mental process. This validation has been suggested by Pritam Singh (1978). Nagpal (1983) has empirically established it and the arrived results had confirmed it further. The whole discussion pertains to the positive relationship of objectives of achievement to the creativity components.

Creativity and Memory

There is relationship of creativity components to **Memory.**

The results had shown that memory is significantly related to the creativity and its components. The results also revealed that there is a gradual decrease in the relationship of memory to the components of creativity (r=.34, .21,.23 for pre-test scores and r=.31,. 19 and .29 for post-test scores).

Memory is the lowest cognitive ability, on the contrary creativity is the higher mental process. Therefore, memory and creativity components revealed a differential position in hierarchial model of cognitive learning Results clearly suggested that memory is significantly related to the Fluency but its relationship with the higher levels (Flexibility and Originality) of creativity decreases. This shows that persons with good memory are more fluent. Perhaps that is why they are called creamers. In flexibility, one has to shift his mental process from test to the similar available environmental information. So in these cases nor memory but understanding is required. Similarly unusual ideas are required, which are again far away from memory. So, the results are logical.

Achievement and Memory

There is relationship of Achievement to Memôry.

The results in have shown that memory is significantly related to the School Achievement for pre-test scores and for pre-test scores.

The results indicated strong association between achievement with memory, Objectives (Knowledge, Understanding and Application) of Achievement and content have a associated existence. They are part and parcel of mental processes indicating cognitive development. It means any piece of content has a hierarchy of mental process and referring the levels of intellect which are further evaluated with reference to the same. Memory being a lower mental ability has significant and high association with the knowledge, but this association gradually decreases with the higher levels of learning, i.e., Application, with which it has low relationship in comparison to Knowledge. This obviously indicates the hierarchy levels of learning. Therefore, it can be concluded that the following pattern in the hierarchy of learning levels (objectives) exists K,U-A. This has helped us in establishing empirically the relevance of the hierarchy of the objectives to

Memory. This in-fact is also an empirical validation of the constructed test.

Achievement and Self-Concept

School Achievement (SA) to Self-concept.

Data analysis have revealed that self-concept is positively and significantly related School Achievement.

The findings are inconformity with a large number of studies referred to this in Chapter II. All the studies indicated that a high self-concept results in high academic achievement of the pupil on the other hand, with a low self concept pupil generally are underachievers.

Achievement and Socio-economic Status

Results had shown that Socio-Economic Status is significantly related to School Achievements for pre- test scores and for post-test scores.

Several studies had been empirically proved the same (See Chapter II). All the studies had shown significant positive relationship of SES to Achievement. Children belonging to parents of high SES are provided with motivation and good environmental facilities for studies at home as well as outside. Further the lower class environment provides a more restricted range of environmental experiences, which are not conducive to intellectual development. Therefore, higher the SES higher the academic achievement. Hence positive relationship of SES to Achievement is in expected direction.

Achievement and Intelligence

There is no relationship of School Achievement (SA) to Intelligence.

Data analysis have revealed that intelligence is positively and significantly related to the School Achievement for pre-test scores and for post-test scores.

Various studies support the finding, as are reported in Chapter II. The reason is that intelligence is a general mental ability, thus the most important factor of achievement. The higher relationship of both is genuine.

FINDINGS RELATED TO THE VARIANCE IN CRITERION VARIABLES AS EXPLAINED BY EXPERIMENTAL AND CONCOMITANT VARIABLES

The results of Multiple Linear Regression Analysis.

TABLE - 5.1

MULTIPLE LINE A RECESSION ANALYSIS

Criteria Variable	Intercept	Rapp (b1)	OBT (b2)	SC (b3)	M (b4)	SES (b5)	IT (b6)	R½
K	2.60	3.03	-	-.05	-	-	-	.13
		(3.06)		(1.75)				
U	-5.30	5.06	3.82	.082	-	-	-	.19
		(4.00)	(2.88)	(2.20)				
A	.39	1.03	-	-	-	-	-	.03
		(1.71)						
T	-6.57	8.93	5.68	.085	-	-	-	.28
	(5.52)	(3.35)	(1.78)					
F	2.48	2.93	3.19	-	-	-	-	.05
		(1.92)	(2.03)					
X	-2.42	-	1.64	-	-	.085	-	.26
			(3.18)			(1.78)		
O	-7.39	2.50	3.12	.10	-	- -	.19	.26
		(2.84)	(3.34)	(3.78)			(2.90)	
C	-13.55	6.32	8.28	.20	-	-	.30	.22
		(2.82)	(3.47)	(2.90)			(1.83)	
SA	12.96	9.84	9.84	-	0.57	-	-	.37
		(3.55)	(3.55)		(2.06)			

Critical value of t for 5 per cent- 1.986
10 per cent - 1.66

Rapprochement is contributing significantly towards all the Criterion Variables.

Among concomitant variables self-concept, socio-economic status and Intelligence is contributing maximum towards achievement, and creativity. Socio- economic status. Intelligence is contributing towards Originality and creativity.

6

SUMMARY, EDUCATIONAL IMPLICATIONS AND SUGGESTIONS FOR FURTHER RESEARCH

Introduction

Education being a dynamic and continuous process, there are fundamental changes taking place in the objectives, curricular material and teaching-learning process.

Various in service educational programmes of the teachers highlight the fact that there is a need to change the traditional methods, which have been in vogue in primary school since ages. It is hightime, therefore, to realise that the old emphasis on memorisation and rote learning is crippling individual growth. creativity, self-actualisation and self-awareness.

The aim of teaching is to bring out innate potentialities of the child and create such environment so that these abilities are properly cared and nurtured.

The present is an era of science. Every aspect of man's life has been affected by scientific development. Every individual should understand the fundamentals of nature and significance of science in order to lead a whole-some life.

Elementary science equips children with knowledge and understanding of environment. It also helps to develop thinking process which enable them to adjust to their surroundings.

In order to achieve the major objectives of teaching, the mere book reading and rote memory has to be replaced by the strategies which revolve around two phrases i.e. "Science is doing" and "Science is life". Therefore to fulfil the present requirements of nation, creative potential and concepts of different subjects among children should be developed in the classroom, through a systematically organised programme of instructions.

In the study investigator tried to see the effectiveness of two approaches i.e. Rapprochement and Objective Based Teaching in the development of Creativity and Achievement.

Purpose of the Study

1. To study the relative effectiveness of Rapprochement, Objective Based Teaching and Traditional Method of Teaching on the Achievement and creativity at Primary level.
2. To study the relationship of creativity to School Achievement.
3. To study the relationship of memory, self-concept, socio-economic status and intelligence with School Achievement.

To achieve the above purpose the following tasks in a sequence were formulated.

Tasks

1. Construction and standardisation of achievement test.
2. Development of instructional material.
3. Testing experimentally the effectiveness of instructional material.
4. Determining the association of creativity components and School Achievement.

5. Finding relationships of memory, self-concept, socio-economic status, intelligence with School Achievement.

Hypotheses of the Study

1. Significant differences exist among (Rapprochement), (Objective Based Teaching) and (Traditional) method of teaching with respect of Achievement and Creativity.
2. Children taught by Rapprochement show higher scores on Achievement than those taught by the Traditional Method.
3. Children taught by Objective Based Teaching show higher scores on Achievement and Creativity than taught by the Traditional Method.
4. Children taught by Rapprochement show higher scores on Achievement and Creativity than taught by Objective Based Teaching.
5. There is no relationship of Creativity to School Achievement.

Major Findings

Major finding of the study are as follows:

1. The three methods viz. Rapprochement, Objective Based Teaching and Traditional Methods differed significantly from one another in Achievement and Creativity.
2. Pupils taught by Rapprochement achieved higher scores in School Achievement than taught by traditional method.
3. Pupils taught by Objective Based Teaching achieved higher scores in Creativity than taught by traditional method.
4. Pupil taught by OBT scored higher on creativity and children taught by Rapprochement scored higher on Achievement.

5. Creativity is significantly related to Achievement.
6. Memory is significantly related to Creativity.
7. Self-concept is significantly related to Creativity.
8. Socio-economic status is significantly related to Creativity.
9. Intelligence is significantly related to Creativity.
10. Memory is significantly related to School Achievement.
11. Self-concept is significantly related to School Achievement
12. Socio-Economic status is significantly related to School Achievement.
13. Intelligence is significantly related to School Achievement.

Educational Implications

The present study has a number of implications, which if properly appreciated can go long way in appraising the existing position relating to the various components of the educational process. The implications provide the much needed base for its vitalisation, improvement and renewal. For the sake of greater clarity and convenience, these implications are discussed below:

1. *The Curriculum*

At present curriculum development in India lacks direction due to the absence of any theoretical framework. Need for relating curriculum developmental efforts, to basic assumptions underlying, teaching-learning process has yet to be realised by curriculum developers in general and teachers in particular.

According to the rationale of Rapprochement appropriate curriculum can be developed for different subjects and different grades. For appropriate curriculum, development a few important aspects are to be considered 1. Teaching-learning Objectives, 2. Content, 3. Instructional Strategies, 4. Evaluation, 5. Need of the society.

Curriculum can be developed on the rationale of Rapprochement.

2. *Text Books*

According to the rationale of Rapprochement good quality of reference materials including the relevant content should be prepared in the form of books .The content and the evaluation portion should be in tune with the attainment of higher mental abilities. This means that the content should be rich and inculcate higher mental abilities in the learner.

3. *Instructional Material*

The present study has clearly demonstrated the positive impact of Rapprochement and Objective Based Teaching in the development of concepts learning and creativity. Activities on the rationale of Rapprochement significantly help in the development of concepts learning. Demonstrations and experiments related to the content made classroom interaction flexible and make students aware and alert for better learning. Thus improving the teaching-learning process, activities must be pre-planned. The instructional strategies will be helpful in improving teaching-learning process in this context.

4. *Examination*

The evaluation system can be determined on the rationale of Rapprochement. This includes question banks, internal assessment and grading system. Question bank for all the classes as per the mental level of the students can be developed, where the rationale of different objectives of teaching may provide a guideline, with reference to the expected behavioural outcomes. They may prove to be useful in elevating the higher dimensions of learning and thereby total standard of education.

Periodic evaluation is another important aspect. This should be done after a regular interval time (weekly, forthightly, or monthly). Frequent assessment will definitely prove to be helpful in upgrading the standard of education.

Achievement of the students show their performance in a particular area. This can again be graded on the basis of a rationalised system. As per the performance students should be given grades.

5. *Setting and Maintaining Standards*

Standards are nothing, but the levels of expected achievement in terms of obtained scores on some criteria. Rapprochement can be used for this purpose. At primary level to compare the achievement of the children, the objectives in the form of Expected Behavioural Outcomes can be the goal of the teaching learning process. If the objectives are achieved, then they become the focus of teaching - learning process. Again, these objectives can be used to compare standards of achievement in different institutions.

6. *Resource Material and Its Development*

An important application of the study is for the development of various types of instructional, evaluation and self-learning materials. On the basis of Rapprochement various types of activities, experiments and similarly other relevant instructional material can be developed for the development of intellect. Thus, resource material in the form of unit plans with reference to activities and teaching modules can well be framed in accordance with the different categories of objectives. However, this can be in accordance with the complexity of mental process involved, which may further enhance performance in achievement tests.

7. *Learning Experience Its Reorganisation*

Rapprochement can prove a foundation for planning and organisation of learning experiences. Instructions can be geared to the development of intellect. Selection and sequence of learning experiences will however be facilitated in accordance with the developmental process of intellect, not only this but also in conformity with the complexity and hierarchical nature of objectives. Such reorganisation of Objective Based Teaching would ensure good articulation of syllabus. Hence the objective of accountability is automatically covered.

8. *Guidelines for Training Teacher*

Various guidelines can be offered to teacher education for planning in-service education programmes so that teachers can be trained at various levels to achieve the main objectives of teaching- learning. Authorities of colleges of education can offer systematic and constructive procedural processes to make it more effective.

9. *Responsibility of Schools Towards Students of Middle and Lower Class*

Teachers need to understand the values and attitudes that lies behind the behaviour of students coming from middle and lower class families. The teacher should help them in the development of mental abilities, as they do not get proper environment in their families. Teachers need to make concerted and conscious efforts by adopting Rapprochement and Objective Based Teaching. The discussions based on the objects, happenings, play material etc. may provide a smooth interaction among teachers and pupils of all sectors in the development of intellect.

10. *Responsibility and Role of Administrators*

Various methods of teaching and instructions will have no tangible effect unless accompanied by simultaneous coordinated efforts to revise policies, develop curricula, train teachers and modify school organisation. Sufficient concern can be given by administrators for innovations in the field, and to find the effect of an attempted innovation at various levels of educational systems. They should familiarise them with the impact of this model on effective teaching-learning process that accordingly monitor the process of its implementation by teachers in their classrooms.

11. *Development of a Uniform Pattern of Education*

The present study is based on the Cognitive and Behaviouristic theory, thus can be helpful in evolving a uniform pattern of educational system for the harmonious development of our country. On the rationale of both theories appropriate content selection in the form of books, and examination system, based on testing of all mental abilities should be developed. This obviously demands the significant activities based on all the domains of learning. Therefore, effective instructional strategies, should incorporate to meet all above requirements. Uniform pattern of education for all sections can be developed on the basis of this teaching-learning paradigm.

Suggestions for Further Research

The following issues seem promising and important and hence are recommended for further investigation in the light of this paradigm:

1. The present study revealed that Rapprochement of Piagetian Teaching and Objective Based Teaching has proved

its efficacy over the Traditional Method of Teaching. An effort was made to incorporate Piagetian thinking with the Learning Experiences. The Learning Experiences were provided according to the Piagetian thinking considering the age level of the subject. There is need of further researches where this can be incorporated and validated in other cognitive developmental stages as referred by Piaget in various subjects.

2. The concrete examples of existing curricula as per the rationale of Piaget were tried to develop thinking process. There is need to prepare these experiences in the form of activities and tasks for different grades and different subjects, and to validate the same through researches in classroom.

3. The effect of present instructional strategies and paradigm validated is also to be seen for different subjects and classes and at different levels.

4. This paradigm have been proved significant in relation to the development of creativity among children. There is need to explore this further with other groups too. These relationships further need to be tested to verify their relationships.

5. Another important dimension in the research may be to determine the mode of interaction in the classroom corresponding to varied attainment of various objectives in the hierarchy by the students of different level of mental functioning. This would be helpful in the validation of this paradigm of Rapprochement with regard to Objective Based Teaching.

BIBLIOGRAPHY

Abrahamson, A. (1952). "Our Status System and Scholastic Rewards," *Jr. Edu. Social,* 25: 441-50.

Abraham, M. (1974). "Some factors relating to under achievement in English of secondary school pupils", Ph.D. Education, Kerala University.

Allioti, N.C. and W.E. Blanton (1973)."Creative Thinking Ability, School Readings and Intelligence in First Grade Children", *Journal of Psychology,* 84 (1), 137-43.

Anastasi, A. and C.R. Schaefer (1971). "Note on the Concepts of Creativity and Intelligence". *Journal of Creative Behaviour* 5(2), 113-16.

Andreson, J.E. (1960) The Nature of Abilities. In Paul, E. Torrance (Ed.) *Education and Talents*. University of Minnesota Press.

Anderson, J. S. (1964). "A Comparative Study of Chemical Educational Study and Students Ability to the use of Selected Cognitive Processes." Unpublished Doctoral Dissertation, Florida State University, Florida.

Arnold, D. (1973). An Investigation of Relation Among Question Level and Lapse Time". *School Science and Mathematics*, October.

Asha (1989). "A Comparison of Intelligence, Creativity, Achievement and Creative Personality Traits of Central and

Public Schools at Upper Primary Level," M.Ed. Dissertation University of Ajmer, Ajmer.

Atkin, M.C. (1969). "Evaluation Theory Development", *Evaluation Comment* 2, No.1 quoted from Popham, W.J. 1976, *Educational Evaluation*, Prentice Hall International, Inc. 37-38, London.

Ashubel, D.P. (1960). "Educational Psychology: A Cognitive View", New York, Holt Rinenart and Winston.

Banerji, A. (1961). "Influence of Socioeconomic Factors on Academic Achievement". MED. Dissertation, Allahabad.

Bhatia, B. (1961). "Manual Memory Span Test".

Barger, Ben and Hall Evethe (1965). "The Interaction of Ability and Socio-C.S. Variables in the Prediction of College Dropouts and Grade Achievement", *Edu Psycho Measurement,* 25, 501-508.

Barua, U. (1981). "Influence of Capacity of Memorization on Scholastic Achievement" Ph. D. Edu. Calcutta University.

Binet, Affred and Simon (1961). "The Development of Intelligence of Children", Translated by Elizabeth and S. Kote, the Training School ? *Vinoland, New Jersey*, p. 226 quoted by Sanghi, R.S.

Bingham Newsman, A.M. and F.H. Hooper (1975). "The Search for the Wzle Circa 1975; Some Comments on Brainerd's Observations", *American Educational Research Journal;* 12:379-87.

Bingham Newsman, A.M. and R.A. Saunders (1976). "Take a new look at your classroom with Piaget as a guide". *Young Children*, in press.

Binson, V. E. (1942). "The Intelligence and later scholastic success of Sixth Grade Pupil", *School and Society*, Vol. 55, pp.163-67.

Burt (1962). "The psychology of Creative ability", *Burt Edu. Psychology*, 32, 292-98.

Bledsoe, J. (1967). "Self-Concept of Children and their Intelligence, Achievement, Interests and Anxiety." *Childhood Education,* 43, 436-38.

Bloom, Benjamin, S. (1956). "Taxonomy of Educational Objectives: The Classification of Educational Goals". *Handbook of cognitive Domain*, New York, David Mackey and Company, Inc.

Brainerd, J. Charles (1978). *Piaget's Theory of Intelligence, Prentice-Hall*, Inc. New Jersey.

Brookover, W.B. (1962). "Self Concept of Ability and School Achievement I." East Lansing: Office of Research and Publications, Michigan State University.

----------- (1965). Self Concept and Ability and School Achievement II: Improving Academic Achievement Through Students Self Concept Enhancement East Lansing: Office of Research and Publications, Michigan State University.

----------- (1967). Self Concept of Ability and school Achievement III; Relationship of Self Concept to Achievement in High School. East Lansing: Office of Research and Publications, Michigan State University.

Bruner, J. S. (1960). *The Process of Education,* Combridge: M.A. Harvard University Press.

Brunkan, R. J. and F. Sherri (1966). "Personality Characteristics of Ineffective, Effective and Efficient Readers." *Personnnel and Guidance Journal,* 44, 837-44.

----------- "Can We Teach Children to Think Creativity"? Georgia University Athens, Dept. of Educational Psychology, 5 Ap.1972.

Capcin, M.D. (1968). "Self Concept Level and Aspiration and Academic Achievement." *Journal of Negro Education,* 27.

Carlton, L and R.H. Moore, (1966)."The Effects of Self-directive Dramatisation on Reading Achievement and Self-Concept of Culturally Disadvantaged Children." Reading Teacher, 20,125-130.

Cattell, A.K.S. and R.B. Cattell, (1959). "Culture Fair Intelligence Test Scale 2 Form A and B," Institute for Personality and Ability Testing 1602, Coronada Drive Campaign, Illinois.

Cave, R.L. (1970). "A Combined Factor Analysis of Creativity and Intelligence," *Multivariate Behavioural Research,* 177-91.

Centi, P. (1965). "Self Perception of Students and Motivation,"*Catholic Educational Review,* 63, 307-319.

Chadha, N.K. and A.K. Sen (1981). "Creativity as a Function of Intelligence Socio-economic Status and Sex among 12th Grade Students. "*Journal of Education and Psychology,* 52-56, XXXIX.

Chadha, N.K. and Sunanda, (1990). "Creativity, Intelligence and Scholastic Achievement" *Indian Educational Review,* Vol. 25, No. 1-4.

Chopra (1966). "Socio Economic background and failure in High School Examination" *Educational and Psychological Measurements*, 2, p. 495.

Chopra, S. L. (1968) "Measured Intelligence and Academic Achievement as Related to Urban Rural Residence", *Rural Sociology*, 33, 214-17.

Cicirelli, V.G. (1965). "Form of the relationship between creativity, IQ and Academic Achievement, "*Journal of Educational Psychology,* 56, 303-308.

Clifford, J., E. Jack, and Sherman (1975). "Effects of Behavioural. Objectives on Student's Achievement" In ISCS Science Education, 59.2,177-80.

Cline, Richards Abe (1962). "The validity of a Battery of Creativity Tests in a High School Sample." *Educational & Psychological Measurement*, 22, 781-84.

Cohen, J. (1975). "Applied Multiple Regression /Correlation Analysis for the Behavioural Science." Lawrence Erlbaum Associates Publishers. Hills Dale, New Jersey.

Coleman, J. C. (1969) "Psychology and Effective Behaviour"- Bombay : DB, Taraporenla Sons and Co. Pvt. Ltd.

Combs, A.W., D.L. Avila, and W.W. Purkey (1971). Helping Relationships: Basic Concepts for the Helping Professions. Boston: Allyn and Bacan.

Cooley, C.H. (1902). *Human Nature and Social Order*, New York: Charles Seribner & Sons.

Counts, Perry, D.A. (1972). "Study of the Relationship between Academic Achievement and Creativity:" Dissertation Abstract International. Vol 35 (8-A) 4342.

Cropley, A.J. (1965). "The Relationship of Divergent and Covergent Thinking Abilities". *Journal of Educational Researeh. II,* 176-81.

---------- (1966). "Creativity and Intelligence" *Journal of Educational Psychology,* 36-259-66.

---------- (1967). "Creativity, Intelligence and Achievement." *Journal of Educational Researeh,* 13(1) 51-58.

---------- (1968). "A Note on the Wallach Kogan Test

of Creativity." *Educational Psychology*, 38 (2),197-201.

Cropley, A. J. and G. W. Maslaricy (1969). "Reliability and Validity of Creativity Tests" *British Journal of Psychology,* 60(3), 395-98.

Dacey, J. S. and G. F. Madous (1971). "An Analysis of Two Hypothesis Concerning the Relationship between Creativity and Intelligence", *J. Educ. Res.,*64, 214-16.

Dass, R. (1959). "A Study of Imagination in High School Students". *Journal of Education*, 3. 18-33.

Dave and Anand (1973). "Validating the Hierarchy of Education Objectives (Bloom) and Relating it to the Research Reports in Education." Regional College of Education, Mysore.

---------- (1973). "Validating the Hierarchy of Education. Objectives (Bloom) and Relating to the Medium of Instruction of Adolescent of Mysore State". Research Report in Education, RCE, Ajmer.

Dave, P. N. (1976). "Hierarchy in Cognitive Learning" RCE, Mysore.

----------- (1974). "Developing a Cognitive Model of Learning". Teacher Today, Bikaner.

Davidson, H.H. and G. Lang, (1960). "Children's Perceptions of Their Teacher's Feelings Towards them related to Self-perception, School Achievement and Behaviour." *Journal of Experimental Education,* 29, 107-118.

Davis, G. A. and T. L. Belcher (1971). "How shall Creativity be Measured? Torrance Tests. RAT, Alpha Biographical and IQ." *Journal of Creative Behaviour*, 5(2), 153-61.

Day, H. I. (1969). "Curiosity and Intelligence" Two Necessary Conditions for a High Level of Creativity. *Journal of*

Special Education., 3(3) 263-68.

Deo, P. and C.C. Gupta (1963). "A Comparative Study of Self-concept of Arts, Science and Professional College Students". Psychological Studies.

——— (1970). "Self concept and School Achievement." Indian Educational Review, 51, 84-87.

Deo, P. and J. Bhullar, "Relationship of Physical Efficiency to Self concept, Intelligence and Achievement." Psychological Studies I, 56-58. Jan. 74.

Desai, Hari Bhai, G. Bloom's Taxonomy Review of Researches - Indian Educational Review, Vol. XIV, No. I, Jan., 1979.

Deutsch, M. (1963). "The Disadvantaged in the Learning Process." In Passow, A.H. (Ed) Education in Depressed Areas. New York College Press.

Dewal, O.S. (1978). "The Use and Abuse of Behavioural Objective, *Jour. of Indian Education,* NCERT, New Delhi.

Drevdahls, E. (1956). "Factors of Importance for Creativity." *Journal of Clinical Psychology,* 12, 21-26.

Eble Robert, L. (1969). "Encyclopedia of Educational Research". Collier Macmillan.

Edward, A. L. (1971). "Experimental Design in Psychology". Research New Bell Amerind Publishing Co. Pvt. Ltd.

Edward, M.P. and L. E. Tyler (1965). "Intelligence, Creativity, and Achievement in a Non-Selective Public Junior High School," *Journal of Educational Psychology,* 56.2.

Eiseman, R. and N. Robinson (1967). "Complexity Simplicity, Creativity, Intelligence and Other Co-relates." *Journal of Psychology,* 67(2), 331-34.

Ernst, H. and C. Drake (1972). "The lost Appalachians. in D.S. Walls and J.B. Stephenson (Eds)", *Appalachia in the Sixties*. Lexington : University Press of Kentucky.

Felker, D. (1974). "Building Positive Self-Concepts." Minneapolis: Burgess Publishing Co.

Fink, M.B. (1962)."Self Concept as It relates to Academic Achievement." *California Journal of Educational Research,* 13, 37-62.

Frankeb, E. (1960). "A Comparative Study of Achieving and Understanding the High School Boys of High Intellectual Ability". *Jour. Edu. Res.* 53, 172-80

Furth, H.G. (1970). "Piaget for Teachers Englewood Cliffs" J.J. Prentice Hall.

Furth, H.G. and H. Wachs (1975). "Thinking goes to school". *Piaget's Theory and Practice,* Oxford University Press.

Gagne Robert, M. (1966). "Elementary Science: A New Scheme of Instruction." Science, 49-53, 151.

Getzels, J.W. and P.W. Jacson (1962). "Creativity and Intelligence: Explorations with Gifted Students". New York, John Willey and Sons.

Gingberg, C.P. and R.G. Whittemore (1981)."Creativity and Varbal Ability: A Direct Examination of Their Relationship". *British Journal of Educational Psychology,* 38(2),138-39.

Glasser, R. (1962)."Psychology and Instructional Technology" in Glasser, R. (ed). "Training Research and Education." University of Pittsburg Press Pittsburg.

Goyal, R.P., "A Creativity and Teaching Success". A *Review of Research Educational Trends*, Vol. 9. No.1-2, Jan.- Dec., 1974.

Gray, S.W. and R.A. Kalaus, (1965). "An Experimental Pre-School Programme for Culturally Deprived Children." Child Development, 36.

Guilford, J. P. (1956). "The Nature of Human Intelligence" New York, Mgrw Hill.

----------- (1959). "Three Faces of Intellect" American Psychologist, 14, 469-79.

---------- (1962). Factors that Aid and Hinder Creativity. Teachers College Record, 65, 380-92.

——— (1970). "Creativity: Retrospect and Prospect". *Journal of Creativity Behaviour,* 4, 149-168.

Guilford, J.P. and P. P. Christensen, (1973). "The One Way Relation between Creative Potential and I.Q.", *"Journal of Creative Behaviour,* 7.4.

Gupta, B. D. (1968). "Ralationship between Socio-economic Status, Family Size and Intelligence" In S.B. Adval (Ed.): The Third Indian Year Book of Education, NCERT, New Delhi.

Gupta, O.V. (1977). "Intelligence, Creativity, Interest, Frustration as Functions of Class Achievement, Sex and Age," Ph.D., Psy., Agra University.

Harmohan Singh and Smt. Saraswati Singh (1977). "Manual and Directions for Self concept Scale for Children".

Harrow A.J. (1972). "A Taxonomy of Psychomotor Domain." David McKay, New York.

Hasan, P. and H.J. Butcher (1966). "Creativity and Intelligence: A Peartial Republication with Scottish Children of Getzels and Jackson's Study, *Br. J. Psychology,* 57, 129-33.

Hastings, J. Thomos (1966). "Curriculum Evaluation- The

Way of Outcomes." *Journal of Educational Measurement.* 3(1), Sprinting, 27-32.

Herson, J.D. (1971). "The Effect of Behavioural Objectives on Student's Achievement in College Chemistry" *Journal of Research in Science Teaching.* 8,385-91.

Herr, E.L. (1965). "Creativity Intelligence and Values; A Study of Relationships". *Exceptional Children,* 32 (2), 114-15.

Irwin, F.S. (1967). "Sentence Completion Responses and Scholastic Success Failure." *Journal of Counselling Psychology,* 14, 269-71.

Iwata, O. (1968). "Some Relationship of Creativity with Intelligence and Personality Variables." Psychologist, 11, 17-20.

Jain, S. (1965). "An Experimental Study of the Relationship Between Home Environment and Scholastic Achievement, Ph.D.Edu. Agrav.

Jaromllek, John and D. Forster (1981). "Teaching and Learning in the Elementary School." Macmillan.

Johnes Howard, L. and J. Michael Russel (1979). "Hierarchial Learning Paradigm" *Journal of Research in Science Teaching,* Vol.16, No. 6, 489-99.

Jogawar, V. V. "Development of Self-concept in Relation to Some Family factors at Adolescence Level. Ph.D. Nagpur University.

Kammi, Co. and R. Devries (1974). "Piaget for Early Education Progress in the Pre-School in Action". R.K. Parker ended. Bosten.

Kheer, W.A. and P. Abrahams (1962). "Hatstead Brain Impairment, Boldness, Creativity and Group Intelligence Measure", *Journal of Clinical Psychol.* 18 (2) 115-18.

Kheer, W.A. and P. Abrahams,(1962). Halstead: Brain Impairment boldness, Creativity and Group. IT. *Journal of ClinicalPsychol.* 80, 259-66.

Khire (1977). "Education for Creativity" *Journal of Indian Education,* 3-37, 26-30.

Knopp, H. (1964). "Effect of Extrinsic Motivation, Intrinsic Motivation and Intelligence on Creativity: A Factorial Approach." *Journal of Gen. Psychology,* 34, 91-93.

Krathwhol, D.R. *et al., Taxonomy of Educational Objectives,* Hand Book II: Affective Domain David Mackey Company Inc., New York.

----------- (1965). "Stating Objectives Appropriately for Programme for Curriculum and Instructional Material Development." *The Journal of Teacher Education,* Vol. 16, No.1, 83-92.

Kulshreshtha, S.K. (1956). "A Study of Intelligence and Scholastic Attainments of X and XI Class Students in Uttar Pradesh," Ph.D. Phil. All.V.

Kuppuswamy, B., "Manual Socio-economic Status Scale (Urban)," Delhi: Manasayam.

Lambell, P.B., (1966). "Self-Concept and Academic Achievement in Middle Grade Public Children". Dissertation Abstract International, A-27.

Lamy, M. W. (1965). "Relationship of Self-perceptions of Early Children to Achievement in Reading." In I. J. Gordon (Ed.) *Human Development: Reading in Research, Chicago*: Scott, Foresman & Co.

Lavatelli, C.S. (1970). "Early Childhood Curriculum, A *Piagetian Programme,*" NB:Osten: American Science and Engineering. Learing to be: Report of the International Commission on the Development of Education. Paris: UNESCO, 1972, and London.

Lesser, G. S. (1965). "Mental Abilities of Children from Different Social Class and Cultural Group". Intelligence & Ability: Wiseman (ed). Penguin Books.

Lewin, K.A. (1935). "A Dynamic Theory A Personality". New York, Mc Graw Hill Book Company.

Lindquist (1965). Statistical Method. McMillan Publishers.

Lindvall, C.M. (1964). "Defining Educational Objectives." A Report of the Regional Centre, University of Pitsburgh.

Ludwig, D.J. and M.L. Maehr (1967). "Change in Self-Concept and Stated Behavioural Preferences." *Child Development,* 38, 453-67.

Lunzer, E. A. (1976). "An Appreciation of Piaget's Work." In *Psychology and Education* by Varma and Williams, Hodder and Stoughton.

Lytton, H. and A.C. Cotton (1968). "Divergent Thinking Abilities in Secondary Schools", *Br. J. Edu. Psychol.,* 1969, 39,188-90.

Mager, P.B. (1962). "Preparing Objectives for Programme Instruction." Palo Alto Califo: Feron.

Mahendra (1986). "The Efficacy of the Rapprochement of the Genevan Approach and of the New Behaviouristic Model in the Development of Creativity and Achievement with Reference to Some Other Psychologial Traits at the Primary level." Dissertation submitted to the University of Rajasthan, for M.Ed. Degree.

Majumdar, S.K. (1978). "A Comparative Study of the 'High Creative" and the High 'I.Q'. Pupil with Respect of Their

Achievement in Science", Paper Presented at the Indian Congress Session, Ahmedabad.

Malobika, Ganguly (1989). "Socio-economic Status and Scholastic Achievement." *Indian Educational Review*, Vol 24, No. 1-4.

Manis (1958). "Personal Adjustment Assumed Similarity to Parents, and Inferred Parental Evaluations of Self." *Journal of Counselling Psychology*, 22, 481-85.

Manjula (1980). "A Comparative Study of the Traditional versus ACMCL on Science in Relation to Achievement and Creativity at the Elementary Level." Dissertation Submitted to the University of Rajasthan, for M.Ed. Degree.

Marston, A.R. (1968). "Dealing with Lowself-Confidence." *Educational Research*, 10, 134, 138.

Maslow, A. (1954). "Motivation and Personality" New York Harper & Row.

Mayhan Woodrow, G. (1966). "The relationship of Creativity to Achievement and Other Students Variables" Dissertation Abstract International, 27(6-A) 1978.

McNemer (1969). "Psychological Statistics" 4th Ed. Tokyo, Toppan Co.

Mednick, M.T. and E.M. Andrews, (1967). "Creative Thinking and Level of Intelligence" *Journal of Creativie Behaviour*, 1(4), 428-31.

Mehdi and Fatima (1974). "Creativity and Intelligence: Evidence of Present Educational Trends" *Special Issue on Creativity*.

Mehta, P.H. "The Self-concept of Bright under Achieving Male High School Students", *Indian Educational Review*, 3,2, 81-86, July 1908.

Meyers, A. and P. Kay, (ed.), (1991). The Pennsylvania State University 135 pp. Adviser Robert Shringley.

Meyers, E. (1975). "Self Concept, Family Structure and School Achievement A Study of Disadvantaged Negro boys," Doctoral Dissertation, Teachers College, Columbia University.

Michand, Norman T. (ed.) D. University of Bridgeport 1990 117 pp. chair-person Leo Mann.

Michael William (1950). "Measuring Educational Achievements," McGraw Hill, 118-22.

Miller, T.W. (1973). "Male Self-esteem and Attitudes Toward Women's Roles". *Jour. of College-Student Personnel,* 14, 402-406.

Murphy, T.R. (1973). "Investigation of a Creativity Dimension", *Education Testing Service,* Princeton, New Jersey.

Nagpal S. (1983). "A comparative study of the Effect of Piagetian Pattern of Teaching and of the ACMCL on Achievement of Primary Students with Reference to Some of Their Personality Traits." Submitted to Delhi University for the Doctoral Degree in Education.

Naidu and Aaron, SES. (1969)."Academic Achievement and Intelligence". *Jour. of the College of Education,* Karnatak University, Dharwar, Vol. VII.

National Policy on Education *1986* New Delhi, Ministry of Human Resource Development, Government of India, (Department of Education) May, 1986.

Owen, F.P. (1973). Quoted from Sohan and Celia Modgil. "Introduction to the Application and Piaget's Theory to Education". *Piagetian Research, Compilation and Commentary,* Vol. 4.

Padma, M.S. (1972). "Teaching and Teacher Behaviour : A Trend Report Second Survey of Research in Education." Editor: M.B. Buch, *SERD*, Baroda, India, 78, p. 397.

Paney, H. and Horrocks. "Creativity in a Troop of Low Average Intelligent Boys Scouts". *Adolescents,* 26,231-41.

Paramesh, C.F. (1977). "Creativity Intelligence and Academic Achievement." *The Educational Trends*, 8, 1-4, 129-37.

Pathak P. (1962). "Exploratory study of creativity and Intelligence and Scholastic Achievement." Psychological Studies, (111-9).

Pathani, R.S. (1990). "Psycho-Social Developmental Stage, Self evaluation (Self-concept) and Need Self Actualising-as predictors of Academic Achievement." *Indian Educational Rewiew*, Vol. 25, No. 1-4.

Pavlov, I.P. (1927). "Conditional Reflexes" Translated by G.V. Amrep, London, Oxford University.

Piaget, J. (1951). "The Right to Education in the Modern World." In *UNESCO Freedom and Culture*, New York, Columbia University Press.

——— (1952). "The Origin of Intelligence in Children,, New York, International University Press.

——— (1970). "Science of Education and thc Psychology of the Child " New York, Orion.

——— (1980). "Le Motion De Justice Chez.U. Educational Internationale" In Quatriema Course Pourle Personnel Enseignant: Geneva: Bureau International Education.

Piers, E.Y. (1960). "The Identification of Creativity in Adolescene." *Journal of Educational Psychology,* 51., 346-51.

Popham W.J. (1967). *Educational Statistics for the*

Behavioural Sciences. McGraw Hill Book Co., New York 272-73.

Popham W.J. (1968). "Probing the Validity of Arguments Against Behavioural Goals" In Anderson, R.C., et.al, Current Research Prentice Hall.

Pritam Singh (1977). "An Investigation into the Empirical Validaties of Bloom's Taxonomy of Educational Objectives". An unpublished Doctoral Dissertation, Delhi University, Delhi.

Purkey, W.W. (1970). "Self-concept and School Achievement." Englewood Cliffs, N.J. Prentice Hall, Inc.1970.

Pushpo, M. (1980). "Social Deprivation and Cognitive Development of Primary School Children" Social Change Osmania University.

Raina M.K. (1968). "Study of Some Correlates of Creativity in Indian students" Ph.D. Dissertation, University of Rajasthan, Jaipur.

---------- (1969). "A Study of Sex Difference in Creativity in India." *Journal of Creative Behaviour,* 3(2), 111-114.

Rais, Ahmed and A.V. Jafri : An Experiment in Creative Teaching. And The Educational Trends, Vol. 8, Nos. 1-4. Jan-Oct, 1973.

Ram Kumar, V. : Self-concept and Achievement in School Subjects of Prospective University entrants, Ph.D. Edu., Ker, U.

Rastogi, K.G. (1964). "A Study of the Relationship between Intelligence, Interest and Achievement of the High School Students", Ph. D. Edu. Raj.U.

Ripple & May (1962). "Caution in Comparing Creativity and I.Q. " *Psychol. Reports*, 229-30.

Rogers, C. (1959). "Counselling and Psychotherapy: Theory & Practice". New York: Harper & Raw.

----------- (1969). "Freedom to Learn." Collumbus, Ohio: Merrill Publishing Company.

Rosen Bernard C, and D'Andrale Ray, (1959). "The Psychological Origins of Achievement Motivation", *Sociometry*, Vol. 22, pp.185-218.

Sandeep, P.P. (1978). "Classroom Interaction and Cognitive Development in Primary School Children". Unpublished Ph.D.Thesis. Osmania University, Hyderabad.

Sandhu, Tej Singh "Does Creativity Influence Academic Achievement?, *Journal of Indian Edu.* Sept, 1976.

Saini, B.K. (1977). "Academic Achievement as a Function of Economic Status and Educational Standards of parents" *Psychological Studies,* 22,2, pp. 24-27.

Sarswat, R.K. "Self Concept in Relation to Adjustment, Values, Academic Achievement, Sexs and Sex of High School Students of Delhi, " *Indian Educational Review*, Vol - 20, No.3, July.1985.

Scheirer, M.A. & R.E. Krant (1979). "Increasing Educational Achievement Via Self-concept Change." *Review of Educational Research*, 49, 131-50.

Schilcht, W.J. Jr. (1968). "Creativity and Intelligence : Further Findings" *Journal of Clinical Psychol;* 24 (4) 458.

Shavelson, R.J. (1981). "Statistical Reasoning for the Behavioural sciences" Boston: Allyn & Bacon.

Shaw, M.C. & D.L. White (1965). " The Relationship between Child Parent Identification and Academic Achievement." *J. Clinical Psychol.* XXI.

Siegal (1955). *Non-Parametric Statistics for the Behavioural Sciences*. Mc Graw Hill Book Co., New York.

Simpson, E.J. (1966). "The Classification of Educational objectives: Psycholmotor Domain." *Urbana* I II: University of Illinois, July, 1965. May 31.

Skinner, (1968). *The Futurology of Teaching.* N.Y. Appleton Crofts.

Smith, A.B. (1965). "An Analysis of the Scealability of Knowledge and Comprehension Levels of Toxonomy of Educational Objectives." American Educational Research Association, Chicago, February.

Springbelt, B.M. (1957). "An Approach to the Measurement of Creative Thinking." *Chand J. Psychol.* II 9-20.

Stedman, C.H. (1973). "An Analysis of the Assumptions underlying the Taxonomy of Educational Objectives: Cognitive Domain. " *Journal of Research Science Teaching.* 10, 3.

Storr, Anthony (1972). "The Dynamics of Creation," Pelican Book.

Sultan, E.E. (1962). "A Factorial Study of the Domain of Creative Thinking".*British Journal of Educational Psychology,* 3378-82.

Thorndike, E. L. (1949). *Selected Readings from a Connectionists Psychology*, Appleton Century Crofts.

Tyler, R.W. (1964). "The Relation Between Recall Higher Mental Process". In C.H. Judd. *Education as Cultivation of the Higher Mental Processes*, Macmillan, New York, 6-17.

Taylor, C.W. (ed.) (1964). *Creativity, Progress and Potential*, New York, McGraw Hill Book Co. 241.

Taylor, C and J. Holland (1964). "Predictors of Creative Performance." In Taylor C.(Ed.) *Creativity Progress and*

Potential, New York, McGraw Hill, 141.

Treffinger, D. and J. B. Huber (1975). "Designing Instruction in Creative Problem Solving; Preliminary Objective and Learning Hierarchies." *The Journal of Creative Behaviour*, 9-4-260-66.

Torrance, E.P. (1962). "Torrance Tests of Creative Thinking" *Norms Technical Mannual* (Research Education).

———— (1973). "Improving Predictions of the Adult Creative Achievement of Gifted Girls by Using Autographical Information". *Gifted Child Quarterly*, 91-95.

———— (1965). "Different ways of Learning for different kinds of children." In E.P. Torrance and R.O. Storm (Eds.) *Mental Health and Achievement*, New York, John Wiley and Sons, 253-62.

———— (1965a). *Rewarding Creative Behaviour*. Englewood Cliffs, N.J.O, Prentice Hall, Inc.

———— (1967). The minnesot a studies of Creative Behaviour: National and International Extensions". *Journal of Creative Behaviour*, 137-54.

Uname Lange Rech (1980-81). "Self-concept, School and Social Setting", *Jour. of Educational Research*, Vol, 74 No.16.

Vanita (1985). A Comparative Study of the Effect of Thinking Games and Objective Based Teaching on the Development of Creativity and Achievement in Dissertation Submitted to the University of Rajasthan for M.Ed. Degree.

Vasantha, R. "An Investigation into the Relationship of Size of Family of Self-concept and Academic Achievement." *Education and Psychology Review*, XII, 3-4, 107-113.July-Oct., 1972.

Vasantha, R. (1973). *Self Concept and Achievement*, Trivandrum, Radha Publications.

Vernon, P. E. (1969). "Intelligence and Cultural Environment" Methuen.

Verma, B.P. and Asha Tiku (1990). "Effect of Socio-economic Status and General Intelligence". *Indian Educational Review,* Vol. 25, No. 1-4.

Vinod (1991). "A Comparative Study of Rural / Urban Teachers on the Measures of Intelligence, Self concept, Creativity, Level of Aspiration of Their Respective Students".

Wade, S. (1968). "Differences between Intelligence and creativity." Some speculation of the role of Environment." *Journal of Creative Behaviour,* 2(1) 97-101.

Watson, J.B. (1924). *Psychology from the Stand-point of a Behaviourists* (2nd ed.).

---------- (1925). *The Ways of Behaviourism*. Harper and Row.

Walbesser Henery, H. (1964). "Evaluation as a Guide to Course Improvement".

Weikart, D. P. (1973). "Development of Effective Pre School Programme: A Report on the Results of high/ *scope-y. psilant* - Pre-School projects, Paper presented at the High SchoolEducation Research Foundation Conference, Ann Arbor, Michigan.

William, R. and Rutherford, (1972). "Differential Teacher Regard for Creative Students and Achieving Students (California)". *Journal of Educational Research,* 1972 (March) Vd. 23(2), 89-90.

Yadav, R.S. (1989). "An Advanced Theory of Cognitive Learning". An Experimental Study through Leacture and guided discovery methods Psycho-lingua.

Yadav, J. (1980). "An Exercise Testing a Piagetian Type Task". Unpublished Manuscript, University of Pittsrburg.

Yamamato, K. (1962). "A Study of the Relationships between Creative Thinking, Abilities of Fifth Grade Teachers and Academic Achievements. Doctoral Dissertation." University of Minnesota, Minnepolis. (Dissertation, Abstracts 23:2801: University Microfilms order No. 63-1873)1965.

Validation of Tests of Creative Thinking : A Review of Some Studies. *Exceptional Children*, 1965, 31-281-90.

Zaide, Rehana (1989). "Scholastic Achievement of Primary School Children", Effect of parental deprivation and Socio-psychological factors. *Indian Educational Review*, Vol. 24. No. 1-4.

Zimmerman, I. L. and G. Allebrand (1965). "Personality Characteristics and Attitudes Towards Achievement of Good and Poor Readers". *Journal of Educational Research* , 59, 28-30.

APPENDIX - I

LESSON PLAN:

(Based on the Rationale of Rapprochement of Piaget and Behaviourism)

UNIT : MATERIAL AROUND US
TOPIC : STATES OF MATTER
CLASS : III
TIME : 35 MINUTES

INSTRUCTIONAL OBJECTIVES:

1. Students acquire the knowledge of terms; Matter, Solid, Liquid and gas.
2. Students develop understanding of (1) define solid liquid and gas and (2) cite examples of different solid, liquid and gas.
3. Students apply the knowledge and understanding gained to explain the interrelationship of the 3 form i.e., Solid, Liquid and Gas and how these three forms help to solve practical problems like, What is water Cycle.

CONCEPTS:

1. All the things present in the universe can be termed as 'matter'.
2. The matter exists in three forms - Solid, Liquid and Gas.
3. Things like ice are solid things.
4. Things like water are known as *liquid things*.
5. Things like steam are gasses.

INSTRUCTIONAL MATERIAL:

Beaker, Spirit Lamp., Ice pieces, and Wax.

INTRODUCTION:

Teacher asks following questions to the students.

Q. What things do you see in your surrounding?

Expected Answer- Students name the different types of things, e.g., Chair, tree, fan, animals, water etc.,

Q. What thing is present in the classroom which is not seen but we can feet of it only?

Expected Answer- Air

TEACHERS STATEMENT:

All the things like-tree, table, blackboard, bus, well, gas can be termed as matter. Therefore matter includes the things of different kinds, shapes, sizes, from a minute particle of sand to the giant mountains. Thus whole matter exists in three forms. Today we shall discuss it under the topic of 'States of Matter'.

EBOs (Expected Behavioural Outcomes)	LEs (Learning Experiences)	RLOs (Real Learning Outcomes)
Pupils-		
Observed Carefully	Tea cher performs an experiment to show the three forms of matter. He takes few ice pieces in a beaker, shows tothe students and then put it on the lighting spirit lamp and asks.	
Hypothesis that at will boil or get heated.	What shall we be getting by heating ice pieces?	
Recognise that steam comes out of it on boiling.	What do you see when it is boiling?	
	The teacher repeat the experiment with wax.	
Generalise		What is water cycle?
	Tea cher sketches a diagram on the black-board showing ice, water and steam and asks.	
Pridict out that water exists in three forms i.e., water and steam.	What are the various forms of water?	

	Teacher statement-these three forms of water i.e., water, ice and gas are respectively known as solid, liquid and gas.	
Define that things like ice are solids. Define the things like water are known as *liquids*. Define the things like steam are known as *gasses*.		What is solid? How will you define liquid? What is gas?
	Tea cher statement- Now you have understand that matter exists in three forms,solid, liquid and gas	
Cite examples of Solid materials Cite examples of liquids Cite examples of gaseous material.		Give some examples of soild-material. Name some liquid things. Name some gaseous material.

APPENDIX - II

LESSON PLAN OBJECTIVE BASED TEACHING

UNIT	:	WEATHER
TOPIC	:	WATER - CYCLE
CLASS	:	III
TIME	:	30 MINUTES

INSTRUCTIONAL OBJECTIVES :

1. Students acquire the knowledge of the terms: Water, water-vapour, rain, clouds, water-cycle.
2. Students develop understanding of the functioning of the water-cycle and the interrelationship of the various terms acquired.
3. Students apply the knowledge and comprehension, thus acquired in solving such unfamiliar but related problems, such as the functional use of water-cycle in the daily life.

CONCEPT:

1. Weather is description of atmospheric conditions prevailing at specified time of place. With respect to heat, cold, rain or sunshine.
2. Water that goes into the air is known as *water vapour*.
3. The cyling of water earth to air from ponds, rivers, etc.,and then back to earth through rain is known as *water- cycle*.
4. Water-vapour from clouds and clouds given rain.

TEACHING AIDS:

Chart Showing Water - Cycle

INTRODUCTION :

Sometimes, it is cool and pleasant in the morning. At other times, it rains in the morning, but becomes sunny at noon. We often say it is very cold today, or it is very hot. Today we will discuss as to what do we mean when we say these things, i.e., we will discuss about weather.

EBOs (Expected Behavioural Outcomes)	LEs (Learning Experiences)	RLOs (Real Learning Outcomes)
Pupils:		
1.1 Recognise that it is raining outside.	1. Teacher referes to the weather outside and asks: (i) What type of day are we having today?	
1.2 Recall that is was a sunny day yesterday.	(ii) What type of day did we have yesterday?	
1.3 Give hypothesis that air, water, or sun is being talked about.	(iii) What are we talking about when we say that it is a sunny or a rainy day?	
Student listen carefully	2. Teachers Statement: When we say that it is sunny we say that it is sunny or a rainy day or a very hot or a very cold day, we actually describe the weather.	
Student Generalise		How will you describe weather?

Contd./-

EBOs	LEs	RLOs
1.4 Reason out that water dries up after sometime from there.	If you spill water on the floor or on your shirt, what do you use after sometime?	
1.5 See-relationship that the cloth does not remain wet after sometime.	If you apread a wet cloth outside does the water remain in it after sometime?	
Listen-	The cher statement: Water does not remain in either the wet cloth or shirt or on the ground after sometime.	
1.6 Hypothesise that it becomes steam, vanishes, goes towards the clouds or air and so on.	Where does this water disappear?	
1.7 Hypothesise that it will boil or get heated. Student Hypothesis	When we heat water, what will happen to it? Tea cher statement: When water boils, steam is formed. What it formed when it dries up? Teacher clarified their hypothesis by the following statements.	

Listens and note down on their note-books.	When water dries up from any open surface a ground or a wet cloth, it becomes water-vapour.	
1.8 Infer that water from them will also dries up.	What will happens to water in the ponds, or rivers?	
1.9 Generalise that water from any open surface will dry up.	Will the water from wells and streams also dry up?	
1.10 Predict that heat from the sun dries this water.	Why does this water dry up?	
1.11 Infer that water goes into the air.	Where does this water disappear?	
1.12 Recall that on drying up, water that goes into the air becomes water vapour.		That does this water become in the air?
	Teacher statement. Since it was cloudy that day, the following question was asked with reference to it.	
1.13 Recall/Recognise that clouds are seen floating in the sky.	What do you see floating in the sky on a rainy day.	

Contd./-

EBOs	LEs	RLOs
1.14 Generalise that clouds are made up of water.	How are clouds formed?	
1.15 Predict that this water comes from the ponds, lakes and rivers.	From where does this water come?	
1.16 Interpret that it reaches the clouds in form of water-vapour.		How does water from ponds and rivers reach the clouds?
1.17 Predict that rains return this water to earth.	Do we got back this water?	
1.18 Interpret that clouds give rain.	How do we get rain?	
1.19 Students Generalise. Students Observe, listen and note down in their note books.	Tea cher Statement Teachershows a chart on water cycle and explains the given Water that goes into the air is returned back to the earth. This is the water cycle.	How are clouds formed? What do you understand by the water-cycle Explain.

APPENDIX - III

UNIT PLAN (PURE BEHAVIORAL)

Unit - Weather

S.No.	Concepts/Facts	No.of lessons	Time required	Scope of Contents	Teaching aids
1.	Water-cycle	1	35 minutes	a. Concept of weather b. Evaporation of water from open surface such as lakes. c. Rivers, formation of water-vapour d. Formation of clouds e. Formation of rain f. Cycling of water from earth of air and air to earth.	Chart,showing water cycle.
2	Forms of Water	1	35 minutes	a. Water has three forms: (i) Solid (ii) Liquid (iii) Gas b. Coversion of one form of water to another.	

Contd./-

Appendix III (Contd.)

S.No.	Concepts/Facts	No. of lessons	Time required	Scope of Contents	Teaching aids
				c. Melting of ice and experiment regarding ice.	
3.	Factors responsible for evaporation of water.	1	35 minutes	a. Sun b. Wind c. Changes in weather due to water cycle	Charts showing relation of weather and water cycle.
4.	Importance of weather in daily life.	1	35 minutes	a. Information about weather b. Knowledge of weather to a farmer navigator or a pilot.	Pictures, cuttings and charts.

APPENDIX - IV

LESSON PLAN

(BASED ON THE RATIONALE OF RAPPROCHEMENT)

UNIT : FORCE, WORK AND ENERGY.
TOPIC : FORCE
CLASS : 5TH
TIME : 40 MINUTES.

INSTRUCTIONAL OBJECTIVES:

1. Students would be able to recall the definition of force and force of gravity.
2. Students would be able to develop understanding :
   a. To cite examples of force and force of gravity.
   b. To discriminate between force and force of gravity.
   c. To genralise different situations.
3. Students would be able to infer, predict and hypothesis the concept regarding force and force of gravity.

CONCEPTS:

1. A push or pull is called *force*.
2. Force make the objects move and stop the moving objects.
3. The downward pull of the earth is called the *force of gravity*.

INSTRUCTIONAL MATERIAL:

Ball, toy car, toy engine, piece of chalk and the student example.

INTRODUCTION:

Teacher put a toy car on the table and push it, the car starts moving, toward another direction then he/she stops the car by another hand and say, like this many things arounds us move and stop. What makes the objects to move or to stop? We are going to study about this.

EBOs (EXPECTED BEHAVIOURAL)	LEs (LEARNING EXPERIENCES)	RLOs (REAL LEARNING OUTCOMES)
PUPILS: Observe carefully	Teacher again put a toy car on the table and ask a student to come and push it and ask:	
Students reason out that when we push a car, it moves.	-What makes a car to move? -Teacher asks two students A and B come over and asks A to push B and ask:	
Students reason out that when A push B, he moves backward.	-What makes B to move backward? Teacher ask B to pull A and asks:	
Students reason out that when B pulls A he moves towards B.	-What makes A to move toward B? TEACHER STATEMENT: It is always pull or push that moves objects. Apush or pull is called *force*	DEFINE FORCE
Students cite examples (By activities)		Show some activities or situations, which indicate that force is applying.
Students observe	Teacher asks a student to come over the stage and to throw a chalk of piece upward and asks	Name some situations where force is used to move objects.
Students reason out that some force is applied on it.	A throws a chalk upward but it fall down. What makes it fall?	

Students predict that this will come come down again. Students generalise it will come down due to some force applied on it.	Teacher again tends to throw a ball upward and asks the students to observe care fully and asks what would happen, when I throw this ball upward?	It will come down.
	Teacher again in asks: Why do all the objects fall or come down to the earth?	Due to some force applied on them.
	TEACHER STATEMENT: Yes, It is a force within the earth which pulls every object down. This downeard of the earth is called the *force of gravity*.	-Define force of gravity? -Give some examples of force of gravity.
Student discriminate Students predict that engine moves	TEACHER STATEMENT: Now you can understand what is force and what is the force of gravity. Teacher shows a toy engine and push it and asks: What happen when I apply force?	-When an object is thrown from a high, Why does it fall? -What is the difference between force and force of gravity?

APPENDIX - V

LESSON PLAN

(BASED ON THE RATIONALE OF OBJECTIVE BASED TEACHING)

UNIT	:	FORCE, WORK AND ENERGY.
TOPIC	:	FORCE.
CLASS	:	5
TIME	:	40 MINUTES.

INSTRUCTIONAL OBJECTIVES:

1. Students would be able to recall the definition of force and force of gravity.
2. Students would be able to develop understanding
   - (a) to cite example of force and force of gravity.
   - (b) to discriminate between force and force of gravity.
   - (c) to genralise different situations.
3. Students would be able to infer and predict the concept regarding force and *force of gravity*.

CONCEPT:

1. A push or pull is called *force*.
2. Force make the objects move and stop the moving objects.
3. The downward pull of the earth is called the *force of gravity*.

INSTRUCTIONAL MATERIAL:

Chalk, Blackboard.

INTRODUCTION:

You all see many things around us move and stop what make the object to move or to stop?

EBOs (EXPECTED BEHAVIOURAL OUTCOMES)	LEs (LEARNING EXPERIENCES)	RLOs (REAL LEARNING OUTCOMES)
PUPILS: Reason out that engine moves the train Reasons out that by pushing or pulling we can move an object. Reason out that we push the ball with foot. Reason out that we pull to open the door. Reason out that we push the door to open it.	**TEACHER'S STATEMENT** You see many things around us move. Trains run on railway tracks. What makes it move? How can you move an object? When you kick a ball. What do you do? How do you open the door? How do you close a door? **TEACHER STATEMENT:** All the example show that it is always push or pull that move objects. A push or pull is called *force*.	What is force? Name some situations where force is used to move objects.
PUPILS Reason out that it comes down. Reason out that leaves fall on the ground. Generalise that some force is applied to them.	**TEACHERS ASKS:-** When you throw a ball upward, what happens? Where does the leaves fall from the trees? Why do all the objects fall or come down to the earth? **TEACHER'S STATEMENT:-** It is a force within the earth which pulls every object down. This down	Define force of gravity. Give some examples of force of

EBOs	LEs	RLOs
Define force	ward pull of the earth is called the *force of gravity*.	gravity.
Discriminate that apull or push is called *force* and the downward pull pull of earth is called *push*.	Now you are able to understand that what is force and force of gravity.	When an object is thrown from a hight why does it fall? What is the difference between force and force of gravity?
Reason out that the goal keeper stop the ball in his hand.	**TEACHER ASKS:** How does goalkeeper stop the ball?	
Reason out that we catch gulli with our hands.	How do you catch a gulli?	
Reason out we catch ball with our hands.	How do you catch a tennis ball?	
Generalise that we can move an object by applying force.	How can you move an object?	
Generalise that we can stop a moving objects by applying force in opposite direction.	**TEACHER'S STATEMENT:-** When you apply force on an object, it can move and when you apply force on an moving object, It may stop if force is applied in opposite direction.	
Students predict that if we apply force on an moving object in the direction of its movement, the object will move fast.	**TEACHER'S STATEMENT:** When you apply force on an object in the direction of its movement, the object will move fast.	What will happen if you apply force on an moving object in the direction of its movement? How can we change the direction of a moving object?

APPENDIX - VI
Achievement Test

NAME ____________________

CLASS ____________________

ROLL NO. ____________________

SECTION ____________________ M.M.50

SCHOOL ____________________ Time. 40Min

In the following four alternative answers are given for each question, chose the most correct answer and write the alphabet a,b,c or d in the bracket given -

1. Which of the following animals give birth to off springs
   (a) Horse (b) Rat (c) Tiger (d) All the above. ( )
2. If you grow a plant in a dark room with only a small hole on the wall.
   (a) The roots will grow towards the hole.
   (b) Only flowers will bend towards the hole.
   (c) The stem will bend towards the hole.
   (d) The stem will bend away from the hole. ( )
3. What happens to a cockroaches when light is suddenly flashcd.
   (a) They move towards the light.
   (b) They move away from the light.
   (c) They do not move.
   (d) They run in all directions. ( )
4. What will happen if your hand come in contact with a hot object.
   (a) We withdraw our hand.
   (b) We hold the thing tightly.
   (c) We do not react.
   (d) None of the above.

5. Lime water turns milky when we blow into it, because
   (a) The air we breath out contains carbon dioxide.
   (b) The air we breath out contains oxygen.
   (c) The air we breath out have no gas.
   (d) None of the above. ( )
6. What would happen if the trees found at high mountains are not conical in shape.
   (a) The snow would be deposited on the trees.
   (b) They will not look beautiful.
   (c) They number of trees would be increased.
   (d) None of the above. ( )
7. Energy is released when -
   (a) Oxygen reaches different parts of the body.
   (b) The food is burnt.
   (c) The absorbed food reaches different parts of the body.
   (d) The absorbed food is broken down by oxygen. ( )
8. Camel is able to walk on sand because -
   (a) It has long leg.
   (b) It has long neck.
   (c) It has padded feet.
   (d) None of the above. ( )
9. Desert plants generally have spine like leaves as -
   (a) They look beautiful.
   (b) They reduce the loss of water.
   (c) Desert plants grow naturally in desert.
   (d) None of the above. ( )
10. What helps a frog to live in water -
   (a) Sticky skin.
   (b) Webbed feet.
   (c) Specific body shape.
   (d) None of the above. ( )
11. Which of the following features help the animals found in cold places to withstand extreme cold weather -

(a) Sharp horns.
(b) Body colour.
(c) Thicky wooly coat.
(d) None of the above. ()

12. Which of the following is an example of hinge joint
(a) Knee joint.
(b) Joints in the skull bones.
(c) Joints in the back bones.
(d) Joints in the shoulder bones. ()

13. Skull bone is so hard and strong because -
(a) It protects the brain.
(b) It gives shape to face.
(c) It protects the heart.
(d) None of these. ()

14. If a person does not wear proper shoes and does not walk properly, what would happen -
(a) It would cause flat foot.
(b) It would cause deficiency disease.
(c) It would cause communicable disease.
(d) None of the above. ()

15. Bone cage is useful as -
(a) It gives shape to our body.
(b) It protects internal organs.
(c) Both (a) and (b).
(d) None of the above. ()

16. If the backbone of a person is consists of a large number of immovable bones, the person -
(a) Will not be able to bend backward and forward.
(b) Will be able to bend backward and forward.
(c) Will not be able to stand.
(d) None of the above.

17. What is the best way go get the daily requirements of vitamins-

(a) Eat at regular time.
(b) Take several vitamin pills.
(c) Eat a balanced diet.
(d) Get lots of sleep. ( )

18. How can you increase the food value of grains
(a) by frying.
(b) by steaming.
(c) by sprouting
(d) by roasting on fire. ( )

19. A child has cracks at the corner of his mouth, red and raw tongue, pain, numbness and loss of sensation is the limbs, what deficiency disease is the suffering from -
(a) Vitamin A.
(b) Vitamin B.
(c) Vitamin C.
(d) Vitamin D. ( )

20. Rickets can be prevented in a child by giving him -
(a) Plenty of fruits.
(b) Exposure of sunlight.
(c) Food rich in Vitamin A.
(d) Food rich in Vitamin C. ( )

21. At present, there is no vaccination for preventing -
(a) Diptheria.
(b) Malaria.
(c) Polio.
(d) Tuberculosis. ( )

22. A child has pale and colourless lips and flat nails, what deficiency is the suffering from -
(a) Anaemina.
(b) Vitamin A.
(c) Vitamin D.
(d) Vitamin C. ( )

23. If there is a case of communicable disease in your family, what would you do -
(a) Keep the infected patient in a separate room.
(b) Keep his belonging clean.
(c) Take vaccination.
(d) All of the above. ( )

24. What would happen if you eat the food exposed to flies -
(a) It may cause typhoid.
(b) It may cause polio.
(c) It may cause tuberculosis.
(d) It may cause Rickets. ( )

25. What measures would you suggest to reduce the soil erosion in a piece of land -
(a) Planting of trees.
(b) Terracing.
(c) Constructing bunds.
(d) All of the above. ( )

26. The running water carrier rich soil and deposit it in the river bed, This is called -
(a) Silting.
(b) Erosion.
(c) Deposition.
(d) None of the above. ( )

27. What would happen if the cutting of tree would be increased-
(a) Soil erosion would be increased.
(b) Soil erosion would be decreased.
(c) It would not affect the erosion of soil.
(d) None of the above. ( )

28. Pollution of air is due to -
(a) Burning of conventional fuels.
(b) Smoke given out by automobiles and factories.

(c) Cutting of trees.

(d) All of the above. ( )

29. Air consists of -

(a) Oxygen.

(b) Nitrogen.

(c) Carbon Di-oxide.

(d) All the above. ( )

30. When you suck a liquid with a straw it is filled with the liquid because -

(a) The pressure of air reduces in straw.

(b) The pressure of air increases in straw.

(c) Neither the pressure increases nor decreases.

(d) None of the above. ( )

31. We can prevent pollution of air -

(a) By planting more trees.

(b) Automobiles should be checked to reduce the release of harmful gases.

(c) Factories are advised to treat the chemical waste and gases before discharging in the air.

(d) All the above. ( )

32. When we push an empty bottle in the water and then tilt it, the air bubbles come out because -

(a) The empty bottle actually contains air.

(b) The water contains air bubbles.

(c) Air bubbles come out from the atmosphere.

(d) None of the above. ( )

33. The force of gravity alone is acting when -

(a) A car is running on the road.

(b) A camel is pulling the cart.

(c) A child pulls another child.

(d) A ripened fruit falls on the ground. ( )

34. To walk on a very smooth surface is difficult than on a less

smooth surface because -
(a) The surface has low friction.
(b) The surface has high friction.
(c) There is no friction at all.
(d) None of these. ( )

35. We can move an object by -
(a) Reducing friction.
(b) Applying force.
(c) Increasing friction.
(d) Changing shape. ( )

36. What would you do to reduce friction in a sewing machine
(a) We should oil it.
(b) We should increase the speed.
(c) We should decrease the speed.
(d) None of the above. ( )

37. What a goal-keeper do in football match to stop the ball -
(a) He applies the force against the direction of ball.
(b) He applies the force in the direction of ball.
(c) The ball stops at its own.
(d) None of the above. ( )

38. Rotation of earth causes -
(a) Days and night on sun.
(b) Days and night on earth.
(c) Days and night on moon.
(d) None of the above. ( )

39. Which of the following is an example of solar energy -
(a) River water falling from a height to move turbine.
(b) Gas produced by cow dung and other excreta.
(c) Moving of wheel by wind.
(d) Solar cooker. ( )

40. What would you advise to lift a heavy load easily -
(a) A pulley.
(b) A crane.

(c) Scales.
(d) None of the above. ( )

41. The lever makes work easier because work is -
(a) divided into small parts.
(b) Done with machine.
(c) Done with the help of handle.
(d) Spread over a large distance. ( )

42. What would you use to split a log of wood -
(a) A lever.
(b) A wedge.
(c) A Screw Jack.
(d) An inclined plane. ( )

43. Which of the following materials should be used to make the front portion of driver's seat -
(a) Wood.
(b) Iron.
(c) Glass.
(d) Plastic. ( )

44. Shadow formation depends upon -
(a) The size of the object.
(b) The size of the source of light.
(c) The distance between the object and the source of light.
(d) All the above. ( )

45. Solar eclipse occurs when -
(a) Shadow of earth falls on the moon.
(b) The earth is in the shadow of the sun.
(c) The moon and the sun becomes invisible.
(d) None of the above. ( )

46. Which of the following situations can cause an accident -
(a) Playing with fire.
(b) Playing on the roads.
(c) Not following traffic rules.
(d) All the above. ( )

47. What would you do if you get a simple cut -
    (a) Cut should be washed.
    (b) It should be covered.
    (c) See a Doctor.
    (d) All of these. ( )
48. Green revolution means -
    (a) An increase in dairy products.
    (b) An increase in the yield of many crops.
    (c) Both (a) and (b).
    (d) None of the above. ( )
49. National Park and Sancturies are places where -
    (a) Wild animals are hunted.
    (b) Wild animals are protected.
    (c) Plants are protected.
    (d) None of the above. ( )
50. We should protect plants and animals because -
    (a) They are beautiful to look at.
    (b) Add to beauty of the surroundings.
    (c) Maintain balance in nature.
    (d) None of the above. ( )

APPENDIX - VII

Development of Cognitive Learning through Integrated behavioural and Genevan Strategies in the Classroom*:

An Indian teacher educator has been experimenting with many indigenous and borrowed Western models of teaching. During 1970s, attempts were made to convert the Bloomian objective-based evaluation model into an objective-based teaching model called *Advanced Curriculum Model of Cognitive Learning* (ACMCL). The Regional Colleges of Mysore and Ajmer experimented with the Model in their teacher's training programme. The author and her students explored extensively the possibility of integration between the ACMCL and the Genevan Approach for developing cognitive learning in the classroom. This paper reviews the salient results of their efforts in the paper.

The aim of institutional education at any level is to provide varied learning experiences through various methods/media/learning situations. Generally, objectives of eduction, syllabus and textbook are prescribed in our schools. Since it becomes the responsibility of the teacher to cover the syllabus and textbooks during the academic session, She has to convert the content (subject matter) into actual learning experiences. These learning experiences should be concrete, measurable and predictable. They should not only be related with the coverage of syllabus but also be concerned with the general objectives of education, viz, the cognitive development of learners.

The aim of education is an all-round development of the child, i.e. development of physical, mental, social and emotional aspects.

* Also published in *Perspective in Education,* Vol.12, No. 4, 1996.

Technically, they are known as the *Cognitive Psycho-motor and Affective Domains* (Bloom, 1956). No doubt, all domains are equally important, yet it is not feasible for a teacher to develop all these domains in a period of 45 minutes. His/her main concern in those 45 minutes is to provide maximum learning inputs to students to cover a specific portion of syllabus (departmental requirement) and to satisfy their intellectual curiosity. Therefore, s/he has to convert broad educational objectives into specific instructional objectives. These instructional objectives should be such that are attainable in a period of 45 minutes.

Behavioural psychologists feel that learning objectives—intended learning outcomes should be overt, observable and measurable. Learning experiences should be derived from the intended learning outcomes and should be subsequently measured through actual learning outcomes. It is possible for a teacher to provide such learning experiences in their regular teaching that may help in achieving the intended learning outcomes. Therefore, s/he has to deliberately plan her/his lessons in such a way that all his/her teaching comes through concrete stimuli. These stimuli may be questions or demonstrations or anything related to teaching through any teaching aid/mode/media. They should help learners to be active and participatory in the teaching-learning process. The learners must also contribute significantly by their varied responses to the development of a lesson.

Keeping this in view, the Rapprochement Strategy of teaching is discussed here. This strategy is an integration of an Objective Based Teaching (OBT) founded on the principles of the behavioural model called an *Advanced Curriculum Model of Cognitive Learning* (ACMCL) propounded by Dave (1975[2]) and the Piagetian Method of Teaching (PMT) based on the Cognitive Development Genevan Theory. In order to understand, this approach, it is necessary to have a background of both the

Behaviouristic Theory, i.e. ACMCL and the Cognitive Development Theory.

The Behavioural Theory — ACMCL

According to behaviourists, knowledge exists in the external environment and it must be transferred to the child little by little, in a sequential order unit complex ideas/concepts are systematically formed. This view holds as if children have no knowledge of the internal structure available to them and, thus, it is important to simplify and plan carefully each step of the lesson. Instructional strategies based on behavioural principles are more precise and structured. According to this Model, the Objective Based Teaching (OBT) could be used to improve teaching-learning process.

In the ACMCL, learning experiences (processes) are integrated with learning outcomes expected to be attained. This is a model which can easily be used in the actual classroom. It is essentially a modification of the Bloomian Model which has been primarily used for the purpose of evaluation. The ACMCL is a three dimensional paradigm. It contains the input—Expected Behavioural Outcomes (EBOs), Method/Modes/Media—Learning Experiences (LEs) and the outcomes—Real Learning Outcomes (RLOs). The significance of the ACMCL has been emphasised to develop the mental processes through content and multi-way interactions among teachers, students and teaching-learning material. Moreover, the developed mental processes are evaluated side by side through RLOs. This indicates that process and product in teaching-learning process are interrelated.

In fact, the aim of the paradigm is cognitive development through the fact, the aim of this paradigm is cognitive development through the manipulation of subject matter and methods/modes/media. The teaching learning environment has to be organised in such a way that the overall intellectual development takes place according to a planned strategy. This paradigm further assumes that cognitive development does not take place in vacuum or in abstract, it has to be manifested in the teaching-learning process.

The Cognitive Development Theory.

Cognitive Development theorists propound that children's innate mental processes enable them to construct knowledge as they act on their environment. According to the Cognitive Development Theory, knowledge is assumed to reside neither in the environment nor in he organism but to be constructed through the interrelationship of both. Although the development of intelligence (mental process) proceeds spontaneously, yet the present world in which children are born is far from the ideal environment for growing intelligence. We assume that many children enter school, if not with a crippled intelligence, at least with an intelligence that is not well nourished. So the schools should offer such an environment where a child is given freedom to explore environmental things or objects.

The Piagetian Method of Teaching (PMT)

Piaget was the most outstanding exponent of the Cognitive Development Approach to learning. He was concerned with the qualitative changes which take place in a person's mental make-up from birth to maturity (Fourth and Wachs, 1975[3]). He believed that the human organism has a characteristic internal learning. The three postulates, i.e. internal organisation, invariant functions and interaction between organism and environment, are fundamental to Piaget's postulates. His theory deals with the nature and the development of thinking on which any learning can be based. Piaget's main concern in education is to provide a criterion for the development of thinking. He has emphasised the role of play in the cognitive development of children. According to him, games and playful activities are part and parcel of the child's cognitive development. Play is essentially a means of learning.

Accordingly, the first job of our schools should be to strengthen the thinking foundation on which any thing, particularly learning, is grounded. To do this, administrators, teachers and the society at large must come to a fuller understanding of the natural development of the child's mind. Moreover, at the early schooling the aims should be to emphasise and purposefully nourish the thinking capacity of the child, besides making him or her to read and write. Instead of compelling the child to read and write, various playful activities or games should be provided for intellectual development. The development of intellect subsequently promotes the development of learning of any concept. Piagetians believe in providing those experiences that are not directly related to the school learning *per se*. The spontaneously global intellectual development is considered the outcome of the transfer from the related but not identical tasks.

The Piagetian Theory does not directly deal with the desired task and, therefore, is inadequate as it emphasises cognitive development in isolation. In the Indian context, it is very difficult to bring a sudden revolution in the classroom with a notion of shifting the whole classroom into a playground for the purpose of cognitive development only. At the same time, the weaknesses of the traditional method of teaching cannot be ignored, which neglects intellectual development, thereby defeating the very purpose of education in itself. Hence, a need was felt to develop a *via media,* that is, Rapprochement between the Behavioural Theory—ACMCL and the Cognitive Development Theory.

The above discussion of the Behavioural Theory—ACMCL and the Cognitive Development Theory, as well as research conducted in this area, lead us to conclude that both these approaches can be merged into one. As emphasised earlier, objectives, instructions and evaluations are interrelated. Behaviourist aims at the development of intellect through pre-planned objective-based teaching-learning process and material, whereas Piagetians believe in the strengthening of thinking process through various playful activities or games. They believe in providing indirect experience as it is felt that intellectual development is the outcome of the transfer from these indirect tasks.

Nowadays, many researchers are engaged in studying the empirical evidence of Piagetian thinking in the development of intellect. It is felt that many of these efforts are not related directly with the teaching-learning processes of the classroom. In the Indian context, textbooks and curriculum play an important role and whatever is to be done must revolve around that. According to the Behavioural Model—ACMCL, the textbook and curriculum must be manipulated through various teaching strategies. It is difficult to change the whole school environment according to the Piagetian rationale. At the same time, the idea of cognitive development cannot be totally ignored. Therefore, there is a need of evolving such teaching-learning strategies which would aim at the enhancement of global cognitive development. This approach has the potential for thc improvement of classroom instruction, curriculum design as well as for the development of concepts in various subjects along with cognitive development. It is noteworthy that Lunzer (1976) also felt the need of this type of integrated strategy for improving the classroom teaching. He observed:

> One of the principal objectives in the study of Cognitive Development may now be brought about a Rapprochement between Genevan approach and that of New Behaviourists (Bloom, Carroll, Gagne and others). On the one hand, it may be fruitful to view the spotaneous development of operational behaviour as the outcome of transfer from related but not identical tasks. One the other hand, it seems essential

to supplement the kind of hierarchical conceptulisation as envisaged by Gagne, a hierarchy based on relevant previous knowledge by studying the complementary role of the Piagetian hierarchy, which deals not so much with the knowledge relevant to success in a particular task as with the way in which these elements need to be used together to enable the subject to cope with more complex relations.

It is necessary to reiterate that Dave[5] also propounds a hierarchical arrangement of EBOs. Keeping in view the remarks of Lunzer and empirical evidences of a few studies, an effort is made to develop a teaching-learning strategy which will fulfil the requirements of both the Behavioural Model and the Cognitive Development Theory.

Characteristics of the Rapprochement Strategy

1. It is combination of the Objective Based Teaching (OBT) derived from the ACMCL and the Piagetian Method of Teaching (PMT) derived from his cognitive theory.

2. The ACMCL is a three dimensional paradigm. It contains the Input—Expected Behavioural Outcomes (EBOs) Method/Model Media—Learning Experiences (LEs) and the Output—Real Learning Outcomes (RLOs).

3. The PMT can be incorporated at the second level of OBT. In teaching-learning process, a few objectives can be determined as EBOs. To achieve these EBOs, instruction should be undertaken according to the rationale of PMT. The developed concepts may further be evaluated side by side by RLOs.

4. In this manner, the whole content of any subject can be converted into appropriate stimuli-response patterns. Stimulus, according to Piaget, may be an activity of a verbal

question which can stimulate the thinking process of the child and motivate him to take active part in learning.

Empirical Support

An attempt has been made to empirically verify the relative effectiveness of teaching techniques in relation to achievement and creativity of the students. Five different studies were conducted in this direction by—Manjula, 1980; Nagpal, 1982; Vanita, 1985; Mahendra, 1986; and Kour, 1994.

Salient Features of the Studies

— A pre-test post-test experimental control group design was used.

— Sample of 36, 95, 66, 95, and 95 students standards III, III, IV, III and III of both sexes (primary level) were selected.

— The main objectives of the enquiry in all the above mentioned studies were more or less similar as indicated below:

(i) To study the relative effectiveness of the OBT (ACMCL-based) and the Traditional Method of Teaching on science achievement and creativity (Manjula).

(ii) To study the relative effectiveness of the OBT (ACML-based) the PMT (Piagetian) and the Traditional Method of Teaching on Listening Comprehension (LC) and Reading Comprehension (RC) as well as on achievement in Hindi and creativity (Nagpal).

(iii) To study the relative effectiveness of the OBT (ACMCL-based), the PMT (Piagetian) and the Traditional Method of Teaching on Achievement in science and creativity in rural area (Vanita).

(iv) To study the relative effectiveness of the OBT (ACMCL-based), the Rapprochement (Fusion of the OBT and the PMT) and the Traditional Method of Teaching on achievement and creativity with reference to some of their psychological traits, (Mahendra and Kour).

— All subjects were pre-tested and post-tested with the help of the following tools :

1. Achievement Tests (Self prepared).
   a) Achievement Test of Science (Manjula, Vanita, Mahendra and Kour).
   b) Achievement Test of Listening and Reading Comprehension (Nagpal).
   c) The Achievement Test in Hindi (Nagpal)
2. Coloured Progressive Matrices (1975) and Cattell's Culture Free Test Scale II (1959).
3. Torrance Creativity Test (1962, Manula, and Nagpal); Creativity Test by Wallach and Kogan (1962, Vanita); and Test of Creativity by Baquer Mehdi (1985); and Torrance[30] (Mahendra[31] and Kour).
4. Cattell's Children Personality Questionnaire (Nagpal).
5. The Kuppuswamy Socio-economic Status Scale (1973, Nagpal, Vanita, Mahendra and Kour).
6. A scale to Measure Proximity of Mother Tounge (Nagpal).
7. Immediate Memory Span Test of Bhatia, (Mahendra and Kour).
8. Self-concept Scale (Kour).

Findings

The significant findings of the above studies are:

1. The instructional material developed on the rationale of OBT (ACMCL-based) helped in developing all levels of learning measured in term of Knowledge, Understanding and Application in Language, Listening Comprehension and Reading Comprehension, achievement in Hindi and science as compared to that used in the Traditional Method of Teaching. The results of all the five studies were in the same direction.
2. The instructional material developed on the rationale of PMT (Genevan) helped in developing 8 out 9 predictors in the second study (Nagpal) and achievement in science in other studies as compared to that used in the Traditional Method.
3. The instructional material developed on the rationale of Rapprochement helped in achieving higher mean scores at all levels of learning in science than that of the Traditional method of Teaching and the OBT (Mahendra and Kour).
4. The instructional material developed on the rationale of OBT helped in achieving higher mean scores in achievement Tests and creativity components than that developed on the rationale of PMT (Vanita).
5. The instructional material developed on the rationale of OBT helped in achieving higher mean scores on creativity components than that developed on the Rapprochement Rationale of Teaching (Mahendra and Kour) as well as that of in the Traditional Method of Teaching.
6. The instructional material developed on the rationale of Rapprochement Rationale helped in achieving higher mean scores on creativity components than that of in the Traditional Method of Teaching (Mahendra and Koul)

Other Important Results

(i) The Rapprochement strategy was found to be an effective

technique for the attainment go higher scores in achievement, and the OBT (ACMCL-based) was discerned to be an effective measure for the development of creativity.

(ii) Overall results indicate a strong association between content on the one hand, and objectives of achievement and creativity components on the other. Cognitive learning—processes as well as products—developed through instructional strategies—singly and/or integrated—having content of the prescribed syllabus, were tested which indicated a positive relationship between them. Levels of achievement and creativity components are hierarchically related and cumulative in nature. The analysis of data revealed a consistent and systematic increase in the relationship of creativity components i.e. fluency, flexibility and originality to achievement levels.

(iii) While warm hearted students preferred the PMT, students having high intelligence liked the OBT (ACMCL-based) and normal students enjoyed the traditional method of teaching.

(iv) Figural creativity was related positively and significantly to the PMT.

(v) There was a positive and significant relationship of verbal creativity measures with the ACMCL.

(vi) The Traditional Method of Teaching promoted convergent thinking.

(vii) Students belonging to low SES preferred the PMT and those of high SES preferred the ACMCL but there was no correlation between SES and the Traditional Method of Teaching.

(viii) Contribution of the ACMCL and the PMT was the maximum towards Listening Comprehension rather than towards Reading Comprehension.

(ix) The Rapprochement Strategy contributed significantly to all the criterion variables, whereas the contribution of OBT

(ACMCL-based) was only to Understanding and Total achievement in science. Fluency, originality and creativity were also affected.

These results strongly suggest that while OBT (ACMCL-based) and the PMT do help in enhancing achievement and creativity, their hybrid variant—the Rapprochement Strategy may offer more fruitful results. Indeed, the evidence in hand is rather inadequate and, therefore, substantial and sustained further work is needed. However, there is no gain saying that it opens up a promising avenue for exploring the possibility of integrating the two theories that have been believed to be diametrically opposed to each other.

REFERENCES

1. Bloom, B. *Taxonomy of educational objectives: The classification of educational goals. Handbook I — Cognitive domain.* New York: David Mackey and Co., 1956.
2. Cattell, A.K.S. and Cattell, R.B. *Culture fair inteligence tests Scale II — Form A and B.* Coronado Drive Champion, Illinois: Institute for Personality and Ability Testing 1602, 1959.
3. Furth, H.G. and Wachs. *Thinking goes to school: Piaget theory and practice.* London: Oxford University Press, 1975.
4. Lunzer, E.A. An appreciation of Piaget's work. In verma and Williams, *Psychology and Education.* Hodder and Stougston, 1976.
5. Dave, P.N. *Hierarchy in cognitive learning.* Mysore: Regional College of Education, 1976.
6. Manjula. Acomprehensive study of the Traditional versus the ACMCL in relation to achievement and in science and creativity at the elementary level. Unpublished M.Ed. Dissertation, University of Rajasthan, 1980.
7. Nagpal, Shakuntala. A comparative study of the effect of Piagetian Pattern of teaching and other ACMCL on achievement of primary students in language with reference to some of their personality traits. Unpublished Ph.D. Thesis, Delhi University, Delhi, 1983.

8. Vanita A comparative study of the effective of thinking games and the Objective-based Teaching on the development of creativity and achievement in science at the primary level in rural area. Unpublished M.Ed. Dissertation, University of Rajasthan, 1985.
9. Mahendra. The efficacy of he Rapprochement of the Genevan Approach and of the New Behaviouristic Model of the development of creativity and achievement with reference to some psychological traits at the primary level. M.Ed Dissertation, university of Rajasthan, 1986.
10. Kaur, M.J. Effect of intervention on science learning and creativity through certain instructional strategies at the primary level. Unpublished Ph.D. Thesis, Ajmer University, 1993.
11. Raven, J.C. *Colured progressive matrices*. London: Lewis and Co. Ltd., 1975.
12. Torrance, E.P. *Torrance Tests of creative thinking. Norms Technical Manual.* New York: John Wiley and Sons, 1962.
13. Wallach, M.A. and Kogan. *Modes of thinking in young children.* New York: Holt, Reinhart and Winston, 1965.
14. Mehdi, Baquer. *Thinking creatively with word.* Aligarh: Self, 1985.
15. Kuppuswamy. Socio-economic status scale
16. Bhatia. Immediate memory span test. In Bhatia (Ed.), *Battery of performance tests of intelligence.* Poona: Purohit and Purohit, 1961.
17. Singh, H.M. and Singh, *S. Self-concept scale.* Agra: Agra Psychological Research Cell, 1977.

APPENDIX - VIII

TOWARDS TOTAL QUALITY MANAGEMENT*

Of all the factors which influence the quality of educational development, quality, competency and character of teachers, are the most important. 'Deliberate' teacher preparation through teacher education is the need of the day. The need for 'deliberate' education calls for qualitatively proficient teachers. Universalisation of education calls for the need to have such teachers quantitatively in large numbers. Qualitative and quantitative demand for teachers in turn calls for corresponding deliberate provisions to be made at teacher education level. The national objective of producing competent and dedicated teachers can only be achieved through effective Total Quality Management (TQM).

The paradox existing in society and the 'Educational Shpere' call for scientific and innovative review of previous deliberations. The paradox is that as knowledge has exploded, materialistic luxuries have piled up. The happiness and peace in the lives of a common man has been mechanised. Even as the importance of education has been realised by the common man, the standard, status, respect, and the grace attached to teachers has gone down over the years. Education and teacher education have to bear the responsibility for the above paradoxes as both are interrelated.

Research has to be geared to new directions and a global, inter-disciplinary approach is required. There has been a continued concern for improving teacher-education, with several suggestions being made. Surprisingly, however, the problems have persisted. The main reasons for ineffective implementation of the recommendations seem to be the difficulty to undertake massive

* Also published by *Deep Calling*, January-March, 2000.

adjustments in the existing set up and the differing perceptions of those who are expected to implement them. Thus, action initiated through administrative mechanisms has had a limited impact. Various commissions and committees appointed at the central and the state government level in recent decades have all emphasised the need for quality teacher education, suited to the needs of the needs of the educational system.

The quality of teachers education needs to be maintained in terms of the product design and manufacturing process.. In a technical sense; quality in education depends upon the product design (instructional objectives in terms of the competencies to be developed among prospective teachers in behavioural terms). It depends equally upon the manufacturing process (instructional strategies to train teachers), infrastructure process (instructional strategies to train teachers), infrastructure facilities, skill of workers as well as on professionalism of faculty, objective testing procedure and adoption of quality control techniques. Quality further depends on meticulous organisation, congenial working environment, visionary leadership and efficient management in positive human resource development (HRD) climate. Quality is a sum total of a large number of activities which go into the preparation of a product (efficient professional teachers). It has to be built into each and every step of the effort of the institution.

NCTE (1996) has identified ten competency areas: concept, content, context, transactional, evaluation, management as well preparation, collection and use of competency based instructional material, competence in other educational activities, parental contact, and competencies related to community contact and cooperation. Murphy (1992) has also emphasised on competency based teacher education (CBTE) programme. The product design of CBTE should aim to develop among prospective teachers competencies related to subject knowledge, subject application, classroom management, professional development and assessment cum recording of pupil progress. The performance areas for quality teachers are streamlined as performance in the class room, school level performance, performance related to out of school activity, parental contact, community contact and cooperation. Besides this, teachers have a commitment to the learner, to society, to the profession, to achieve excellence, and a commitment to basic human values.

The field experience in teacher education are conducted under a variety of names. Common terms are practice teaching, 'in school' experience, teaching rounds, internship and student teaching. Whatever the name, the essential element of the process is that the student teachers attempt to apply in school setting some of the competencies propounded in the teacher education courses. In fact practice teaching is the single most powerful intervention in a teacher's professional preparation programme. The concept of total quality management must be strictly adhered to in this phase of teacher preparation programme, as it is a powerful intervention in their professional development. Consequently, supervision of student teachers is a very powerful process. In such interventions a large number of resources — physical, human, as well as financial are used, organised and implemented. The quality of product (professionalism in teacher) depends to a great extent upon the management of input (field experiences) to be provided to them during this phase.

Benefits of Field Experiences

We all know that elementary education plays an important role in the development of basic skills of acquisition of knowledge of reading, writing and arithmetic. It help in the development of right attitudes and requisite psychomotor skills. It forms the basic ground for acquiring subsequent levels of education. The need for providing quality elementary education arises from the fact that young children are both depended and impressionable. Inadequately trained teachers are not capable of effecting desirable changes in their pupils. Moreover, better quality education programmes develop such competencies which help them to acquire new competencies during their working life.

The need for a child entered approach in elementary education is being advocated by all concerned. On the other hand, the very structure, design and training methodology of the elementary teacher education programme does not seem to be fully geared for realisation of benefits of this programme. In fact, the status of the current elementary teacher education in the country largely remains confined to traditional and stereotyped method of training. There is a need to improve the instructional strategies in elementary teacher training institutes through which desired teaching competencies could be developed in the pre service student teachers. There is a need of comprehensive networking of innovations to be included in student teaching programmes as they are the weakest link in teacher education.

Practice teaching progamme has been conceived as the most powerful intervention in the teachers professional preparation, but the criticism has crept in because of some of the shortcomings of this programme. The main defects pointed out by different educational researchers and by appraisal of practice teaching of DIETs of four states (Nagpal, 1999) are:

Wide gaps between theory and practice.

Lack of clear-cut objectives of the training programme.

Inadequate institutional training and insufficient input before actual practising in schools.

Indifferent attitudes of the supervisors towards supervision of the lesson.

Disagreement among teacher educators on different issues.

Lack of continuous objective and integrated assessment of the trainees.

Lack of co-operation and support from practising schools.

Wide variation in teaching practice from institute to institute.

Inadequate training in the use of Minimum Level of Learning (MLL), Operation Blackboard or Science and mathematics kits and in the use of multi-media approach.

Poor perception of student teachers towards teaching profession.

Inadequate knowledge of child psychology among teacher educators.

Mismatch between the work experience available in co-operative schools and in institutes.

Lack of purposeful academic support.

Lack of minimum required infrastructure facilities in the physical conditions of co-operative schools. Practice classes being carried on in open spaces with roller boards and in some place in the playground. Classes being sub-grouped in small section to cater to the needs of student teachers and teacher educations, who simultaneously supervise 3-4 student teachers. In such situations, a lot of distraction from one class of the other tends to be routine and completing of the lesson tends to be just a formality.

The elementary teacher education institutes in most of the cases have been started without much preparatory work.

In most cases, the departments are run with a skeleton staff and hence there is a greater reliance on visiting or gues faculty.

The departments/sub units represent more of academic model than professional models.

There is heavy dependence on the concept, case techniques borrowed from other countries.

There has been little emphasis on providing student teachers insight into socio-economic political environments in which Indian schools operate.

The manpower requirements of (manufacturing sectors) Government schools are taken care of too much and in the process, the requirement of other vital sectors (public, urban schools) have taken a back seat.

The linkage between teacher education institutes and varied types of schools has remained weak.

Under such conditions, how the identified competencies of NCTE can be developed, with the inauguration of the planning era, there is an immediate need to develop the management skills, talents and abilities in teacher educators and administrators. Teacher education institutes are unique institutes engaged in exploring, generating, conserving and transmitting the knowledge. It consists of community of students / student teachers and teacher educators who come together, with the goal of learning and expanding the horizons of knowledge. The education under this system is aimed at molding the students into career setting, efficient educational leaders of administrators and especially sensitive organisation leaders cum change agents.

Gap Betweem Teacher Preparation and School Requirements

Consequent to these shortcomings, there arose a gap between teacher preparation and school requirements, the teacher education (student teachers) and the perceptions of teacher education departments regarding the needs of the former, between the service quality specifications as desired by the contemporary school system and the quality of service delivery as rendered in the institutes. A few dimensions of such gaps are between the expectations of customers of teacher education institutes. It is, therefore, imperative of evolve a system of delivery service quality so that teacher education can come up to the desired level of expectations in nearly 430 District Institutes of Education and Trainings (DIETs) which have been established by 1997-98. These institutes are charged with responsibility of organizing pre-service and in-service programmes in addition to being the nodal resource for elementary education at district level. Quality teacher education is expected from these institutes.

Characteristics of Service Quality in Teacher Education

Coller (1999) has rationalised delivering service quality in management education, which is equally applicable to teacher education. He pointed out that service like banking, insurance, education are forming a major part of our modern life. Going by the modified AMA definition, services are those separately idenifiable, essentially intangible activities which provide want satisfaction and are necessarily tied to the sale of products or another service. Providing a service may or may not require tangible good. However when such use is required, these is no ownership in transfer of these tangible goods in a service buying transaction (Stanton, 1981). Teacher education, like management education, fulfils all the key characteristics of a service, viz:

Intangibility : A teacher education undergoing teacher education can only feel about it. Though he watches and participates in the performance of the service, the real output is targeted at his filling.

Inseparability : Imparting of instructions cannot be separated from the teachers of teacher education discipline. Thus the production and consumption of service is highly interactive and interrelated.

Inconsistency : It is not possible to impart teacher education in the same spirit to all the student teachers at the same time. Even if it is rendered, the students may receive it differently.

Perishability : Instructions are consumed as soon a producted and need to be produced every time differently. However, the audio-visual and other devices as instructional support material may guard the instructional aspect of teacher education against this perishability.

Service by their very nature require a different orientation to the market where quality of service becomes decisive. When a service is complete, the customer is not left which a tangible product but rather with feelings like elation, delight, and satisfaction or frustration, disappointment, anger and so on. Providing a quality service must therefore, identify the feeling that the service providers want customers to experience as a result of service.

Fulfilling the need for learning, acquiring the required knowledge, developing the aptitude, professional expertise, skill, etc., are the factor which are going to elate the feelings. Hence a framework of quality and service delivery is the need of the hour in teacher education. Concept of quality in the curriculum framework of teacher education should rotate around the pedagogical philosophical, psychological social rationale of teaching competencies. Practice teaching competencies. Practice teaching is a school based field teaching experience. It is a manufacturing process of the desired competencies. Systematic and determined efforts must be made to develop instructional strategies to strengthen this important component which has the following potential benefits, it its objective are clearly outlined for all concerned.

It will make explicit to both stall and student teachers the skills, knowledge and attitudes, which have often been unstated and half hidden.

It will focus student teachers reflection on their own problems related with the acquisition of teaching competencies.

It will help staff of focus more systematically on whether opportunities are being provided to help student teachers develop compretencies as per the manufacturing design.

It will help to clarify the relationship between subject application and the rationale of developing competencies as per the manufacturing design.

It will improve the transition between initial teacher education and the first year of teaching as per desired competencies.

Instructional Strategy for Quality Teachers

With this background regarding teacher education in general and practice teaching in particular, a Tentative Enriched School Experience Programme for student teacher during practice teaching was conceived by Chetanlal and Nagpal (1999). An action research study was undertaken to develop an instructional strategy for school experience programme in elementary teacher education programme. A need to enrich school experience programme was felt to enable, imbibe and inculcate in the student teacher a sense of purpose and sensitise them to the growing needs of elementary education, receptive to the spirit of child centred approach. With this idea in mind an appropriate instructional strategy was evoled to prepare the target group toward quality teachers for the 21st century.

The study was conducted in two phases, viz., the pilot study (1996-98) and final study (1998-99). The objectives of the pilot study were:

To develop need based lesson plan format to teach all school subjects at the elementary level.

To test the efficacy of the developed lesson plan during internship.

To find out the strengths and weaknesses of existing practice teaching programmes.

To develop instructional strategy in practice of teaching for elementary teachers.

Appropriate scientific procedural steps were followed to achieve the above objectives. The results of the pilot study were very encouraging. Student teachers, teacher educators, supervisors, co-operative school teachers, all expressed satisfaction towards the developed lesson plan as that helped in systematic planning and in the analysis of content in actual teaching-learning process of the classroom through child centred learning experiences.

Student teachers expressed their concern in improving quality of practice teaching through concrete measures. A few such measures were organising practice teaching after sufficient orientation, to have longer duration of practice teaching, development of teaching skills through micro teaching orientation in the development of instructional support material, orientation in peer group observation programme, freedom to experiment with innovative techniques and to have good conducive co-operation from practice teaching schools.

In the light of the above concern of student teachers and deliberations with concerned faculty members, a instructional strategy having four phase for practice of teaching was evolved in a 3 day workshop on "Review of ETE curriculum". The four phases were : the training input, the pre-active phase, the interactive phase and the post active phase.

The Training Input

An enrichment programme as a training input was planned. Various extension lectures and workshops on related topics such as teaching skills, communication skills, micro teaching, writing objective in behavioural terms, theoretical rational behind lesson plan, innovative methods of teaching, first aid, yoga, creative mask making and school readiness were arranged to help student teachers to widen their horizons by learning through participation. A rigorous training input as an instructional strategy was planned after discussion and deliberation with experts in the field. The main features of this strategy were:

Before hand training of teaching skills through micro teaching under simulated conditions for 10 days.

Measurement of entry competency level of school student.

Learning innovative techniques and methods in teaching different school subjects through participation in extension lectures and workshop.

Competency based teaching in the schools by using play-way method in simulated conditions, role-play, demonstrations, discussions and use of puppets, mask and locally available teaching aids in teaching learning process.

Improvement in achievement test report. Gain ratio between pre-test and post-test scores was found and presented through pictorial figures.

Co-curricular activities; with a view to develop organising and managerial capabilities.

Student teachers were given freedom to organise various co-curricular activities related to celebration of important events, festivals and days of national importance.

Managerial skills were developed to handle multilevel abilities in classroom.

Orientation in action research was imparted to develop insight into solving classroom problems scientifically through critical analysis.

Orientation was imparted in peer group observation through the process to recording observations in performa.

Organisating exhibitions in co-operative schools on the day of external evaluation.

The objective of the whole exercise was to provide training input to develop all technical, contextual and interpretative competencies as visualised in NCTE among student teachers. This training input was followed by pre-active phase. The discussions and deliberations on theoretical rational behind lesson planning, writing objectives in behavioural terms and task analysis were part of this phase. It was followed by preparation and checking of need based lesson plans. Demonstration of model lesson plans by experts, faculty and senior peers were organised for the visualisation of actual classroom teaching by student teachers. Interactive phase was the actual teaching practice in co-operative schools. The emphasis was on competency based \ activity based teaching, multi-ability group based teaching, use of innovative techniques, use of action research techniques and use of developed achievement tests by student touchers. The feedback was to provided by the principals \ HMs \ school teachers \ supervisors \ peer group \ investigator at different stages of this phase. Post active phase was the evaluative phase where student teachers analyse the achievement tests and sub, it the records and reports of various assignments.

The instructional strategy so designed was implemented over a period of four months. A set of four questionnaires and attitude scales were administered to find out the efficacy of instructional strategy designed for school experience programme. It was found that this strategy help in achieving the goals of preparing competent teachers for present day schools. However, the focused outcome based on data is given below.

Major Findings

The evolved instructional strategy has implications for equipping student teachers with new approach for professional excellence. The findings clearly indicated the systematic methodological application of innovative activity based learning experience. The instructional strategy designed for field experience programme helped in planning effective management.

1. The training inputs that were provided during school experience programme helped students in developing technical competencies related to the mechanism of teaching-learning process.
2. The preparation of need based lesson plan helped in visualising and organising child entered activities in classroom.
3. The different assignments viz. multiability group based teaching, action research, school plan report etc. helped in developing contextual competencies / related to understanding of school and classroom context.
4. The student teachers organised competency \ activity based teaching in their classroom involving a variety of methods \ techniques and instructional support material.
5. The intense supervision and feedback provided at different stages helped in developing classroom management skills.

The perusal of the above outcomes clearly indicates that there is a relevance of concept of Total Quality Management to teacher education and the goals of school education. Teacher education and management education, have some fundamental similarity (Sapre, 1999). Teachers are manager who are committed to developing prospective pupils through valid knowledge, integrated with personal traits and attributes. Teachers develop their unique styles, which are a blend of knowledge, personal philosophy and personality, derving most of the curriculum content from behavioural science, quantitative science and technology in teaching-learning process.

Total quality means seeing a small part in a big product and a whole global market in a single product. It also means integration of every quality—physical, technical, managerial, economic, social and individual into one organised whole. TQM encompasses both service quality, (process of training teachers) and product quality (usability of trained student teachers as teachers in school education). The quality cannot be achieved effectively without involving people and bringing about global congruence among various work groups, departments and level of management. Any organisation can reach the goal of excellence only when people are empowered and feel responsible.

It clearly indicates that more coordination among teacher preparation programme, monitoring programmes and staff development by institutes of education ad schools is required. Teacher education's task should be comprehensive preparation, which has profound effects on course work and internship. Hence, there is a need for a developmental approach to teacher learning. Student teaching experience, complicated by a relevance of a number of players — a student teacher, co-operating teacher, faculty member — are to be focused to allow students teachers to work within a particular context so that emerging teachers enter their first years of teaching with sound theoretical knowledge and equally sound practical skills. To combat the problems that plague teacher education, a comprehensive agenda is needed for supporting emerging teachers and for extending a range of professional responsibilities — enough to keep the very best teachers engaged in an interesting, stimulating, growth oriented profession.

To have TQM in teacher education some suggestion and strategies have been worked out on the basis of research evidences:

1. **The instructional strategy** for school experience programmes must be made an integral part of elementary teacher eduction institutions.

2. **A need-based lesson plan format** should be provided to student teachers as a guideline. It was found that the preparation of need based lesson plan helped in visualising and organising child centred activities. Lesson plan should be simple, giving clear guidelines and directions for teaching - learning process and should match with actual teaching.

3. **Increased duration of teacher education programmes** to accommodate proper assimilation of the emerging professional inputs. The practising school re to be made an integral part of teacher education institutes. One the basis of supervision, observation and difficulties encountered, it was felt that six month should be for field experience. Appropriate time period for teaching practice is after he first semester since by that time the student teachers would be familiar with theoretical background of pedagogical courses, methodology, teaching skills and strategies, measurement-evaluation etc. Longer period of practice teaching, change of syllabus, minimum 45 minutes duration of timetable is recommended.

During this period, they should act as interns and be under the total supervision of school authorities and teacher educator as a supervisor whose role should be that of a guide. It is acknowledge that formal professional training on continuous basis is necessary for becoming a good teacher as it caters to the development of one's personality and sharpening of communication skills and commitment to a code of conduct. Education of teachers needs to be strengthened and the main attributes of profession such as the systematic theory, rigorous training over a specified duration is required. Conducting diagnostic tests, action research, and achievement tests in practising schools by student teachers during practice teaching may also help the school authorities to improve the quality of education in their schools.

Evaluation criteria of practice teaching should be made available to the students before the commencement of the supervision.

Checking up the lesson play by the peer group instead of supervisors. Supervision and training in observation by the peer group were preferred. Hence this aspect be further probbed for its proper use.

Stress of the teaching practice should be on 7 R's - Reading, Writing, Arithmetic, Rights, Recreation, Owning Responsibility and Conducive Interpersonal Relationships.

Skill and training should be given in multi-grade teaching, school readiness and teaching children with special needs.

Financial incentives in the form of practice teaching conveyance allowance should be given.

New directions in research have to be geared up with global interdisciplinary approach.

4. **Developing a repertoire.** A confirming complex image of teaching is needed that includes a repertoire of techniques for working with children. There is need of stage specific theoretical and practical components, transactional strategies and evaluation. Teachers need a range of strategies for dealing with curriculum, pedagogy, assessment in varied school contexts because schools are different, no technique works every time for all kind. It is to be

acknowledged that good teachers learn new techniques, skills and stategies each year through systematic inquiry, researching, attending seminars and experimenting and reflecting in the company of others. To build a repertoire, teachers need feedback from colleagues with significant expertise.

At the same time, they need to work with the company of other colleagues who are focused on learning the same strategies. One kind of support corrects misuses and misunderstandings, the other provides congenial atmosphere that allows individuals to understand the range of possibilities that any strategy/approach holds. Therefore, pedagogy should be culture specific. Instead of using one uniform mechanistic way of student learning, cultural practices such as story telling, dramatics, puppetry, folk play, community living, etc., should become a strong basis of pedagogy. Sufficient experience and training in the use of play-way techniques for teaching at lower classes, more exposure to instructional material and teaching aids during the internship are required.

In the evolved instructional strategy in action research the process of first two phases viz. The training input and the pre active phase, a sort of repertoire was built, where student teachers learnt new techniques, skills and strategies through systematic inquiry from the organised enrichment programme. More emphasis on initial pre-internship in the institute was given. Training in teaching skills through micro teaching under simulated conditions as well as preparation of instructional support material-cum-audio visual aids, model-cum-demonstration lessons from teacher educators and experts, freedom to experiment with innovative ideas or techniques, training in handling large classes and pupils with special needs, etc. were important components. Prior visits to the schools to establish rapport with the pupils, co-operative teachers and Principals was organised before teaching practice.

However, to make it more successful, allotment of classes before the student teachers, the number of students of the class should be pre-determined. Poor students should be provided with instructional support material like books, pencils and handbooks. Community efforts should be made available to improve the school complex and the classrooms should be provided with environmental infrastructural facilities with the use of innovative techniques and low cost locally available material.

5. **An interconnected system of support.** Once student teachers are learning and building a powerful repertoire, there is a need to connect the pieces that support them. Colleges of teacher education need to collaborate with schools to provide a coherent image of teaching. All parties need to unite active review of their work (Fienman - Nemser, 1999). Intensive involvement of the whole faculty and staff of co-operative schools is required. Systematic supervision of practice teaching through observational schedule incorporating relevant teaching competencies, writing objective comments is required. In America many colleges and Universities engage with school based partners by giving practitioners more responsibility for fieldwork without seriously engaging with practitioners about other programmatic requirements that emerging teachers encounter. Therefore involvement of complete faculty in practice teaching is necessary.

6. **Professional development of teacher educators.** The teacher educators need intensive training in various aspects related to new innovations/techniques like micro teaching, diagnosing testing, action research, multi ability group based teaching/co-operative learning, models of teaching besides organisation of activity/competencies based reaching in pre-primary classes.

The faculty members should be made conversant with new techniques of lesson supervision. The teachers need to be suitably trained and oriented to overcome their crisis of confidence, illusion of non-ignorance, transactional deficiencies and lack of crucial competencies. Action research by them needs encouragement. Tying national goals for teachers to the professional teaching standards can help emerging teachers focus their energies on building on growth programme that is responsive to the pupils they serve and that builds the overall capacity of schools. Mentor teachers skilled in helping teachers assess their skills and progress can also help them understand the resources that exist in education.

Programmes must be available to help new student teachers continue to build their repertoire of an over-expanding set of skills for engaging children in learning. Wesley (1999) cited the case of one of the colleges, where faculty was refreshing course content to prepare teachers to work with children who being all kinds of differences and to demonstrate how technology can be used as a pedagogical and assessment tool. On each course design team, practising teachers examine whether a course content is likely to strengthen an emerging teacher working in her classroom during the initial years of teaching and they develop technological applications for their classrooms that demonstrate course content. The orientation of the principals of the DIETs should be related to administrative aspects and feasibility of implementation of new ideas and techniques in this direction.

7. **Monitoring and support by teacher educators during teacher preparation.** There is a need to build scientific clinical supervision (monitoring) programme in Colleges of Education. The monitoring process during the initial years of teaching should reinforce what it means to be a professional teacher. Reviewing the guidance and support given to student teachers by teacher educators during teaching practice reveals the dire lack of exploring human potential at present. The logic behind teaching practice and feedback is that teacher educators will discern strengths and

weaknesses of student-teachers at every stage of the teaching-learning process, suggest alternatives and provide theoretical explanations for the way a teaching event occurs.

During teaching practice, repeated practice would develop insight into complexities but also stabilise the skills and lead to individualistic style. But a learning plateau is arrived at within 5-6 lessons. A weak style is stabilised. This happens because of pre-specifications - same lesson number, exhibiting specified components, making lesson plans with fixed format, use of same instructional skills and teaching aids. Student teachers feel constrained by the variety of observations by different teacher educators, because feed-back tends to be prescriptive, as if there are some common do's and don'ts in teaching. Quite often details they have to remember bog them down, as do the activities they have to carry out to satisfy the supervisors. Such specifications, instead of enabling a new entrant to recognise what works and adopt the same and refine one's style, constrains exploration of these dimensions. Instead of this, supervisors can help the new teachers reinforce the repertoire of techniques learned during preparation and them supplement that repertoire by adding a new set of strategies.

New teachers need to learn how to learn about their students. They need to learn to use the available data. Too often new teachers build lessons and activities without regard for the students themselves. During the period, they need to get support from experienced teachers who can help them understand how to use data.

Ratio of student teachers / teacher educators to be supervised should be less for proper monitoring.

Mentors need to help beginning teachers to understand that feedback or their teaching is essential to the sound development of a repertoire.

Monitoring programme needs to explicitly help teachers learn that any new approach to curriculum or pedagogy or assessment will have corresponding implications for other dimensions of teaching. With this kind of focused support, new teachers shall have a greater sense of how to organise their professional growth as they begin their teaching career. Participation of school authorities and school teachers in a more intense manner, supervisory feedback, critical review by the supervisor is needed. Supervisors who can work with new teachers during their initial attempt of teaching, and others who can render support to student teachers in crisis are must for quality in teaching.

The need of the hour is to have such teacher educators as mentors who can guide teachers towards excellent teaching standards. Excellence in profession needs teacher's leader who map student's experience with a school to help faculty understand whether the total programme is likely to build students necessary skills. Teacher leaders must build coherence among schools so that all share responsibility for student growth and development. All these roles are needed to build a profession that requires that its mentors mirror what we want for our children : a commitment to a life full of enthusiasm, stimulating and at tines difficult learning. This kind of support it provided for emerging teachers will have long term effects for generations of children. Teacher educators must enable all emerging touchers to build a repertoire that excites children, keeps them engaged and devclops a desire in them to learn more. It should be ensured that newcomers gain the skill not just of being organised, but to give children a lift off toward better learning.

Providing adequate support for emerging teachers requires that teacher preparation be seen as the initial step in building a repertoire. The focus needs to be narrowed significantly to ensure that they are successful in their first teaching. Such a focus should allow college faculty and cooperating teachers to think more deeply about what these teachers need to run their own classrooms with diverse groups of children. For example, these teachers need help with planning, moving children from one activity to another, incorporate children with special needs and focused lessons on skill acquisitions and content knowledge. Such a focus makes teacher preparation more manageable, more immediate and more exciting.

If the present rate of explosion of knowledge continues, in a few years teachers will find themselves in a world where their present knowledge and teaching skills, to an extent, would become obsolete. They will have to face the challenges of the electronic media and information technology and use them meaningfully for educational purposes.

The teacher education curriculum is expected to develop the ten competencies in a teacher who will function in the five performance areas with commitment to the five beneficiaries. How far the present teaching practice of PSTE is meeting the above expectation is adjudged (Nagpal, 1999). The findings of the action research (Neera Chetanlal, 1999) and Wesley's developmental approach are likely to pave the way for policy planners to formulate a quality teacher preparation. It may help to work out strategies to develop ten competencies in a teacher who will function in five performance areas with commitment to the five beneficiaries. The practice teaching needs total overhauling to meet the needs of Total Quality Management (TQM) in teacher education. Rajput (1999) stated the "NCTE" has made its contribution in focusing and highlighting the worth and value of teacher education. Teachers will have to be professionals and their training programme must be characterised by appropriate duration, extended interaction and sufficient rigor". This humble attempt may help to plan a process to achieve the above lofty expectations.

APPENDIX - IX

HUMANISTIC APPROACH TO TEACHER EDUCATION

Context

Curriculum change in teacher education has been long overdue because the existing curricula, which is basically more than 70 years old, has neither changed in substance, nor from nor duration. It has become totally irrelevant both to the actual needs of the profession and to the societal needs for national development. Rohidekar (1996) has rightly remarked that "In the eyes of society teacher education has become a joke and a butt of ridicule as compared to the education of a doctor, engineer, lawyer or even an agricultural officer". NPE (1986) called for a Radical change by saying 'Teacher education shall be overhauled'. Social pressures are compelling us to include "value education, computer education, special education; and importantly management of education - to make teacher education really professional and responsive to the needs of society. Is a classroom teaching 'Trade' or truly 'Professional' in the context of its having 'No Professional Ethics' and No Professional Management Inputs?"

National Council for Teacher Education (NCTE) instead of professionalising the teacher education has adopted a bureaucratic approach to streamline the existing absolute structure with insistence on peripheral infrastructure and the game of numbers. NCTE has to answer and guide how the management of education can be effectively incorporated into the already cramped education system? It is high time that we look around and take a leaf from other professional courses.

---

* Also published by *University News*, Nov. 24, 1997.

Other professional bodies are seriously engaged in modernising and deepening their courses. Internship, an integral part of MBBS courses, in now being implemented in National Law School of India, which already has a 5 year integrated course after plus 2 stage granting a double degree B.A Hons and LLB. The National Law School of India University has to be adopted as the Emerging Model for excellence in teacher education in India. Are we educationists seriously modernising and deepening our courses? An internship which is an integral part of teacher education to be looked into in order to make our teacher education programme effective.

Teacher educators in India have been experimenting with many endogenous and borrowed western models of teaching. During 1970s attempts were made to convert the Bloomian objective-based evaluation model Bloom (1950) into an Objective Based Teaching (OBT) model called *Advanced Curriculum Model of Cognitive Learning* (ACMCL) Dave (1976). The Regional Colleges of Education (RCEs) of Mysore and Ajmer experimented with the model in their teacher training programme. Nagpal (1983) explored the possibility of integration between the ACMCL and the Genevan approach for developing cognitive learning in the classroom. ACMCL is a three dimensional paradigm. It combines the input - Expected Behavioural Outcomes (EBOs), Method/Modes/Media-Learning Experiences (LEs) and the outcomes - Real Learning Outcomes (RLOs). The significance of the ACMCL has been emphasised to develop the mental processes through content and multi way interactions among teachers students and teaching-learning material. Moreover, the developed mental processes are evaluated side by side through RLOs. This indicates that process and product in teaching-learning process are interrelated.

The Genevan Approach emphasises the strengthening of

thinking foundation of which anything, particularly learning is grounded Furti way (1976). Hence at the early schooling the aim should be to nourish the thinking capacity of the child through play way activities/games besides making him/her to read and write.

In the Indian context, it is very difficult to bring a sudden revolution in the classroom by shifting it to a playground for the purpose of cognitive development only. At the same time, the weaknesses of the traditional methods of teaching cannot be ignored, which neglect intellectual development, thereby defeating the very purpose of education in itself. Hence a need was felt to develop a via-media, that is rapprochement between the Behavioural theory - ACMCL and the Cognitive Development Theory PMT. This approach has the potential for the improvement of classroom instruction, curriculum design, as well as for the development of concepts in various subjects alongwith cognitive development. It is noteworthy that Lunzer (1976) also felt the need of this type of integrated strategy for improving the classroom teaching. He observed: One of the principal objective in the study of cognitive development may now be to bring about a rapprochement between Genevan approach and that of new behaviourists (Bloom, Carroll, Gagne and others). On the one hand, it may be fruitful to view the spontaneous development of operational behaviour as the outcome of transfer from related but not identical tasks. On the other hand, it seems essential to supplement the kind of hierarchical conceptualisation as envisaged by Gagne, a hierarchy based on relevant previous knowledge by studying the complementary role of the Piagetian hierarchy, which deals not so much with the knowledge relevant to success in a particular task as with the way in which these elements need to be used together to enable the subject to cope with more complex relations.

It is necessary to reiterate that Dave also propounds a hierarchical arrangement of EBOs. Keeping in view the remarks of Lunzer and empirical evidences of a few studies, an effort is made to develop a teaching-learning strategy which will fulfil the requirements of both the behavioural model and the cognitive development theory.

Nagpal (1996) in her paper "Development of Cognitive Learning through Integrated Behavioural and Genevan Stategies in the Classroom" has discussed the characteristics of the Rapprochement Strategy, salient features and the findings of five empirical studies conducted by her and by her students to verify the relative effectiveness of teaching techniques in relation effectiveness of teaching techniques in relation to achievement and creativity of the students (Manjula, 1980, Nagpal, 1993, Vanita 1985, Mahindra, 1986 and Kour1993). A few most important findings of the above studies are:

1. The instructional material developed on the rationale on rapprochement helped in achieving higher mean scores at all levels of learning in science and creativity components than that used in the Traditional Method of Teaching.
2. Overall results indicate a strong association between content on the one hand and objectives of creativity components on the other. Cognitive learning processes as well products developed through instructional strategies singly and/or integrated having content of prescribed syllabus, were tested which indicated a positive relationship between them. Levels of achievements and creativity components are hierarchical, related and cumulative in nature. The analysis of data revealed a consistent and systematic increase in the relationship of creativity components i.e. fluency flexibility and originality to achievement levels.
3. The Rapprochement Stategy contributed significantly to all the criterion variables.

These results strongly suggested that while the OBT (ACMCl-based) and PMT do help in enhancing the achievements and creativity, their hubrid variant - rapprochement strategy may offer more fruitful results Nagpal (1996). There is no gain saying that it opens up a promising avenue for exploring the possibility of integrating the two theories in teaching practice too in preparing teachers at the elementary level. RIEs of Ajmer and Mysore experimented with the ACMCL model in their teacher's training programme. There is now need to try this model in District Institutes of Education & Training (DIETs)

It is felt that teacher educational institutions are not able to maintain Total Quality Management (TQM) in preparing teachers in this direction. There is lack of dedicated efforts in bringing change and experimenting with new models keeping in view the demands and needs of society. These institutions need a spark of managerial skills of a dedicated leader for their maintenance of TQM. The literature on management revealed that management of any organisation is a highly specialised area, but it is totally neglected in educational sector. The important component of management is human resource development climate which is affecting total quality products. In teacher education, the product is a trained teacher whose quality is to be ensured by teacher educators. During the process of teacher preparation the latest methods of teaching-learning are supposed to be developed. The sufficient practice and drill is to be given in the acquisition of required skills of teaching as an art and science, which is not happening. An attempt was made to have an audit survey of the Human Resource Development Climate of Elementary Teacher Educational Institutions of 16 DIETs of five northern states. The HRD climate is characterised by human touch of joy, care, trust, reward, team-spirit collaboration, feedback and so an among the staff. The relationship among all members is supposed to be very cordial and not hierarchical. There is a need of vision for the institutional mission. The qualitative and quantitative data revealed that the HRD climate of most of these institutions were not so conducive for TQM (Nagpal, 1997).

Teachers are the first and the most effective agents in the long chain of human learning. In some of the major areas, leadership has to play a path breaking role in teacher education concerning the intellectual and attitudinal tuning of its future teachers. The leadership itself, at present, shows pathetic signs of rigidity in terms of curriculum change, insensitivity towards new information, apathy towards the delicacy of human material and mindless authoritarianism. It has to understand that teaching is unlike any other profession where the subject of work is neither inert nor static, but alive human being, suspicious, wilful, impressionable, at the same time autonomous.

The quality of elementary education depends on the quality of elementary teacher education. The student teachers of DIETs, who would be future elementary school teachers are expected to bring out desired changes among the pupils. The major objective of teacher training is to empower teachers to meet the present day challenges by equipping them with necessary competencies of teaching. Elementary teacher education institutions should have adequate inputs to realise the objectives of modern elementary teaching with necessary skills. An attempt was made to explore the input provided in DIETs on the teaching competencies of preservice teachers. A survey of the process of preparing teachers during teaching practice programme was conducted through personal visits, informal interactions, group discussions, interviews and observations. Perceptions/opinions of teacher educators and student teachers were also obtained towards the preparation of teaching practice and internship programme in the cooperative schools, the role and significance of peer-group observation, supervision/evaluation-process, criticism lessons, and towards the importance/relevance of lesson planning etc. (Nagpal 1996). The survey revealed the following:

1. Great variation in the number of phases in the internship/ practice teaching programme in different DIETs (6/3) as
   - First Introduction
   - Micro-teaching
   - Internship in Schools
   - Block-Teaching
   - Criticism-lessons
   - Final lessons/evaluation.
2. Variation in the duration of various phases (10/20/30 days) in various DIETs.
3. Variation in the number of lessons (2/3/5/10) per subject in DIETs.
4. Variation in the number of peer group observation lessons (3/5/10).
5. Lack of written critical comments on the lesson-planning. Supervision of the practice teaching was limited to the writing of the same sentences/phrases on the plan for almost all trainees by supervisors as well as by the headmaster of the co-operative school. In one of the schools, it was found that the headmaster of the school had awarded nine out of ten marks to all trainees.
6. Great variation was observed in the format of the lesson plan on different subjects within and among DIETs. A peculiar mixture of Harbartian Method of lesson planning with that of Bloomian objective-based evaluation system was being followed without any commensuration of the same

with the actual teaching in the classroom.

7. Training of teaching skills was imparted not by doing/ demonstrating, but by lecture method only.
8. Absence of multi-media approach, minimum levels of learning, child centred activity based teaching-learning process/operation black-board (OB) material in the internship programmes.
9. Insufficient staff-strength for the monitoring/supervising of the internship in the schools.
10. Lack of motivation/interest in the teacher-educators in monitoring practice-teaching due to the poor remuneration and transportation facilities.
11. Training methodology used during internship was not commensurate with the guidelines of the DIETs.
12. Multi grade teaching lessons were observed in a few DIETs of Rajasthan. It was discovered that a student teacher was teaching three classes and three different subjects simultaneously. The classroom space was diagonally divided into four. The total 45 minutes period was divided into 9 phases. In five minutes three subjects and three classes were being covered either by person or through instructional material or through exercises/activities. After every minute the student-teacher was shifting her role for all the three classes. Classroom teaching of the student teacher was a ditto replica of the lesson plan, which was kept at the back of the class for the observational comments of the supervisor. It was very surprising that the teacher educator was able to discern the matching of the teaching and the lesson plan from the time of the watch. The efficacy of such teaching strategies in the other states and in the field needs to be tested.

On the basis of above findings, it is essential to have a

standard guideline procedure for the internship programme, where the format of lesson plan for all DIETs as a guide is given alongwith the number of lessons to be delivered per subject, number of lessons to be observed by peer-group, number of lessons in multi grade teaching, duration of phases in the internship programme etc. Training in the use of multimedia approach, OB science kits, MLL based teaching-learning process is required.

The findings of these isolated research studies led the author to conclude that in order to achieve the goal Education For All in the context of development in education, the first target should be achieving the TQM in preparing teachers. The standard process of practice teaching programme as per the guidelines of the DIET should be worked out under the mangerial skills of academic leaders. The academic faculty of DIETs should be provided an academic autonomous psycho-social environment where they feel free to experiment with new teaching practices as well as experience the joy of sharing with their fellow faculty under the academic support of their leader. This academic environment will automatically radiate the young inquisitive minds of would be teachers who are already bubbling with energies to do something great as future nation builders. In this receptive environment the latest research based innovative practices be made available in the library through research journals and other periodicals. Necessary clerical support system should be made available as and when required. It should be made very clear that the development of thinking minds of teacher is not thwarted by any type of block, either human or physical. There is a dire need of human touch to support educational skill development in such a way which one grasps and reflects the specificities of Indian culture and responds to the needs and demands raising from the modern world at the same time. It is empirically found by Sabharwal and Nagpal (1997) in the case-study/biographical research of innovative primary school teachers that in schools, the success, development and sustainability of innovative ideas depend on teacher's efforts and interests in connecting schooling with life in the local community. The making of teacher requires the development of institutions, where body and mind can be formed on natural laws and not on prejudices of the various schools of thought. Humanistic approach does not need costly organisations in order to start its constructive work. It can utilise those already existing provided they are rejuvenated with affectionate human touch. The success of this depends upon the attitude of the administration, which is to look after this basic psycho-social need in making a man. All these things are possible if teacher education system in the country takes a lead and incorporate the above concepts in their theories and practices of preparing teachers with due recognition to human touch as a basic need. There is a dire need of preparing training modules in teacher education programme keeping in view these concepts.

REFERENCES

Bloom, B.(1956) : Taxonomy of Educational Objectives; The classification of Educational Goals. *Handbook 1-Cognitive Domain.* New York; David Mackey and Co.

Dave, P.N.(1976) : *Hierarchy in Cognitive Learning*, Mysore, Regional College of Education.

Furth, H.G. and Wachs (1976) : *Thinking Goes To School : Piaget's Theory and Practice*. London; Oxford University Press.

Kour, M.J.(1993) : Effect of Intervention on Science Learning and Creativity through certain Instructional strategies at the Primary Level. Unpublished Ph.D.Thesis. Ajmer University, Ajmer.

Lunzer, E.A.(1976) : An appreciation of Piaget's Work in Verma and William's. *'Psychology and Education.* Hodder and Stougton.

Mahendra (1986) : The Efficacy of Rapprochement of the Genevan Approach and of the New Behaviouristic Model on the Development of Creativity and Achievement with reference to some psychological traits at the Primary Level. M.Ed. Dissertation, University of Rajasthan.

Manjula (1980) : A comparative Study of the Traditional versus the ACMCL in relation to Achievement and Science and Creativity at the Elementary Level. M.Ed. Dissertation. University of Rajasthan.

MHRD (1986, 1992) : *National Policy on Education.* New Delhi'.

Nagpal, S. (1996) : Development of Cognitive Learning through Integrated Behavioural and Genevan Strategies in the Classroom. *Perspective in Education.* Vol. 12, No.4. A journal of the Society for Educational Research and Development.

________, (1996) : A Study on Human Resource Development (HRD) Climate in Developing Values in Teacher Education (A Focus on DIETs) A paper Presented at the C.I.E. Tenth Annual Conference at D.A.V.College of Education for Women, Amritsar from Nov. 3 to Nov. 5,1996.

________, (1983) : *A Comparative Study of the Effect of Piagetian Pattern of Teaching and of the ACMCL on Achievement of Primary Students in Language with reference to some of their Personality Traits*. Ph.D. Thesis. Delhi University, Delhi.

________, (1997) : *Teacher Empowerment and Human Resource Development Climate.* A paper presented at the 1997 Northern Regional seminar on Teacher Empowerment and School Effectiveneness at the primary Stage at Regional College of Education, Ajmer from 14 to 16 April, 1997.

Rohidekar, S.R. (1996) : *Values and other Dimensions in Teacher Education.* A paper read in the C.T.E. Tenth Annual Conference at D.A.V. College of Education for Women, Amritsar from 3 to 5 Nov., 1996.

Sabharwal, N. and S. Nagpal (1997) : Empowerment of Primary School Teachers - Profiles of Selected Innovative Teachers. A Paper presented at the 1997 Northern Regional Seminar on Teacher Empowerment and School Effectiveness at the Primary Stage at the Regional College of Education, Ajmer from 14 to 16 April, 1997.

Vanita (1985) : A Comparative Study of the Effect of Thinking Games and the Objective based Teaching on the development of Creativity and Achievement in Science at the Primary Level in Rural Area. M.Ed. Dissertation, University of Rajasthan.

INDEX